The Effect of Supply Chain Management on Business Performance

The Effect of Supply Chain Management on Business Performance

Milan Frankl

BEP BUSINESS EXPERT PRESS

The Effect of Supply Chain Management on Business Performance

First published in 2018 by
Business Expert Press, LLC
222 East 46th Street, New York, NY 10017
www.businessexpertpress.com

ISBN-13: 978-1-94744-163-7 (paperback)
ISBN-13: 978-1-94744-164-4 (e-book)

Business Expert Press Supply and Operations Management Collection

Collection ISSN: 2156-8189 (print)
Collection ISSN: 2156-8200 (electronic)

Cover and interior design by Exeter Premedia Services Private Ltd., Chennai, India

First edition: 2018

10 9 8 7 6 5 4 3 2 1

Printed in the United States of America.

Abstract

Supply chain management (**SCM**) is the process of managing the operations of a system of organizations, people, activities, information, and resources involved in efficiently moving products or services from suppliers to customers. SCM can effectively conduct the movements of physical items, knowledge, and information from the original supplier to the final end-user.

In this book, we explore the systemic analysis of SCM and its effect on business development performance. We identify the structural problems in the supply chain, clarify how they influence the functioning of business development, and suggest elaboration of strategic approaches to address those problems.

Professional perspectives and insights resulted from experts including various SCM sources.

Keywords

business development performance, operations management, products and goods movement, supply chain management

Contents

Acknowledgment

I would like to thank Yen Kuo Joe Chiao, MBA, my graduate student at University Canada West, whose research on SCM between China and Taiwan inspired this book. The examples relating to those two countries result from his research.

CHAPTER 1

Supply Chain Management Concepts

SCM Definition

The Council of SCM Professionals (**CSCMP**) defines SCM as follows:

SCM encompasses the planning and management of all activities involved in sourcing and procurement, conversion, and all logistics management activities. Importantly, SCM also includes coordination and collaboration with channel partners, which can be suppliers, intermediaries, third-party service providers, and customers. In essence, SCM integrates supply and demand management within and across companies. SCM is an integrating function with primary responsibility for linking major business functions and business processes within and across companies into a cohesive and high-performing business model. It includes all of the logistics management activities noted above, as well as manufacturing operations, and it drives coordination of processes and activities with and across marketing, sales, product design, finance, and information technology.

—CSCMP*

Introduction

SCM is not a new concept about technology, software, or business systems. In light of the important problems and potential opportunities created by globalization, the high demands on companies to establish systematic relationships with stakeholders are prominent. The tremendous pressures from customer satisfaction, cost cuts, and fast services are essential to shift from the traditional concepts on logistics or marketing channels to

---

* http://cscmp.org/

a comprehensive SCM system. Back in 1915, Arch Wilkinson Shaw[†] was hired by Harvard University to teach business policy, reorganize curriculum, and start the school's Bureau of Business Research. He was the first one to analyze market distribution issues. He published in August 1912, in the *Quarterly Journal of Economics*, an article titled "Some Problems in Distribution Market," which became a seminal article in marketing studies. The business book he wrote and published by Harvard University Press was later considered the world's first textbook on SCM.

"The most pressing problem of the business man today, 'Shaw wrote,' is systematically to study distribution," by which he meant both physically supplying a product and creating demand for it among consumers via marketing.[1]

More than 100 years later, businesses in every industry are working harder to source raw materials globally, manufacture products with lower cost, operate processes more efficiently, move products faster, and better satisfy their customers.

To face the oncoming era of globalization, companies have to accept these challenges. They must take chances to deal with all kinds of tasks by using various strategies and approaches. As Shaw wrote, "Systematic study must replace experiences and empirical rules."[Ibid] This is a precognition, which has forecasted the importance of SCM.

In the global economy, some businesses are increasingly forced to shift from multinational to becoming transnational.[2] Businesses that can locate their suppliers diversely, execute manufacturing operations efficiently, motivate their employees' loyalty capably, transport the goods in a timely fashion, and service their customers satisfactorily are going to be the winners in the present fast-expanding economy.

Each element listed previously is essential to a company's success. However, many companies fail because they do not recognize SCM as an

---

[†] **Arch Wilkinson Shaw** (August 4, 1876–March 9, 1962) was an American management theorist, editor, and publisher, who applied the ideas of scientific management in the areas of offices and the tertiary sector. He was also Secretary of Commercial Economy Board and member of the board of directors of the Harvard Business School, during the First World War. (https://en.wikipedia.org/wiki/Arch_Wilkinson_Shaw)

essential contributor for the profitable accomplishment of their business development.

Air Canada, for instance, had many long-term problems related to its operations, financial management, networking, pricing, union issues, and customer service. Even though other airlines were also struggling to cope with the travel slump caused by the September 11, 2001 attacks, the war on Iraq, and stiff competition at that time, Air Canada was doing poorly while Singapore Airlines was doing well.[3]

Therefore, to figure out how to improve a business core advantage and to increase its strategic competitiveness, SCM is becoming more critical, especially in a global business setting.

SCM Revisited

According to the Canadian Supply Chain Sector Council,[‡] SCM encompasses the planning and management of all activities involved in sourcing and procurement, conversion, and all logistics management activities. Importantly, it also includes coordination and collaboration with channel partners, which can be suppliers, intermediaries, third-party service providers, and customers. In essence, SCM integrates supply and demand management within and across companies.

SCM as an integrating function has a primary responsibility for linking major business functions and business processes within and across companies into a cohesive and high-performing business model. SCM includes all the logistics management activities noted earlier as well as manufacturing operations, and it drives coordination of processes and activities with and across marketing, sales, product design, finance, and information technology.[§]

What Is a Supply Chain?

A supply chain is the sequence of organizations, their facilities, functions, and activities that are involved in producing and delivering a product

---

[‡] http://supplychaincanada.org/en/
[§] http://supplychaincanada.org/en/supply-chain

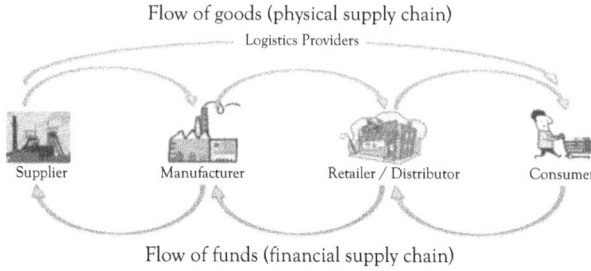

Figure 1.1 Flow in a supply chain

Source: CTMfile.com

or service. The sequence begins with the suppliers of raw materials and extends all the way to the final customers as end-users of the product or service provided. Facilities include factories, processing centers, warehouses, distribution centers, retail outlets, and offices. Functions and activities include forecasting, purchasing, inventory management, information management, quality assurance, scheduling, production, distribution, delivery, and customer service.[4]

Figure 1.1 illustrates the physical information flow between various entities in a supply chain.

Dr. Douglas M. Lambert defines SCM as "The integration of key business processes from the end user through original suppliers that provides products, services, and information that add value for customers and other stakeholders."[5]

Business Practice Management

Business practice management (BPM) is closely related to SCM. The whole approach to BPM was systematically introduced in the 1980s. BPM is a business strategy intended to help companies overcome the challenges of fluctuating markets and adapt to the ever-evolving needs of consumers. BPM operations are associated with various scientific researches and technological advances, which can manage effectively the supplier's selection, manufacturing process, transportation arrangement, logistical availabilities, and customer satisfaction issues. BPM also involves a variety of activities on sourcing raw materials, manufacturing products, scheduling shipment, warehousing and distribution, quality control, and customer service, all part of a series of complicated systems, in which every step in their links must be executed with adequate delivery, quality, coordination, and performance at the right time, the right place, and the right cost.

Since the 1990s, when technology started to drive the marketplace and the informational revolution speeded-up business, companies in every industry were encountering important challenges about how they could manage their issues with superior competitiveness under fierce competition. Many of these companies, especially international enterprises, began to pay more attention to their business strategies to compete against their rivals for business development.

They found that to beat their counterparts, it was not enough to improve only their efficiencies and quality within their organizations. They also had to cooperate with their partners as a single entity and develop a comprehensive supply chain, which could assist them in becoming more competitive in the marketplace. The understanding and practice of SCM has become an essential prerequisite for staying competitive and boosting business profitably and market share.[6]

In current business settings, SCM has been identified as a comprehensive integration of different forms of operational management. If a business were to operate without an effective SCM practice, that business would be vulnerable to competition, which might lead to a reduction of effectiveness, sustainability, and profitability.

The Digital Revolution

The **Digital Revolution** representing the change from mechanical and analog electronic technology to digital electronics began anywhere from the late 1950s to the late 1970s with the adoption and proliferation of digital computers and digital record-keeping that continues to the present day.

In 1994, Netscape was the first company attempting to capitalize on the newly introduced World Wide Web (**WWW**).[5] The release in 1995 of version 1.0 of the Internet Explorer by Microsoft, introduced in earnest the WWW to the business world. Many companies started to capitalize

---

[5] https://en.wikipedia.org/wiki/Netscape#Early_years

on e-commerce and e-business by using the Internet for their supply chain. Manufacturers, for example, with better information exchange, could forecast their demand of mass production by earlier arrangements for raw materials, labor, and facilities. Retailers, with better cooperation with their suppliers, could also keep their safety stock levels in check to meet their customers' needs by applying practices on third-party logistics, quick response, inventory control, and price-setting efficiently.

Under extensive application of information technology, many companies found that they can improve their multiple-service capabilities by integrating in more effective ways their internal systems with those of their external partners. Thus, innovations and updated approaches were developed to strengthen production, distribution, inventory, packing, and transportation.

Newer information technologies including management information system (**MIS**), radio frequency identification devices (**RFID**), decision support systems (**DSS**), electronic data interchange (**EDI**), and other knowledge-based systems (**KBS**), have significantly improved supply chain progress in business problem-solving.[7]

Components and types of information systems (IS) have expanded significantly to include a wide variety of elements and concepts as technology cost reductions made them more affordable to big, medium, and small businesses. (See Figures 1.2 and 1.3.)[8]

Some researchers have associated these improvements with the supply chain and proclaimed the arrival of a **New Economy**,[9] as a transition from a manufacturing-based economy to a service-based one. Some of the old rules regarding the trade-off between unemployment and inflation appear no longer to apply. Productivity advancements brought on by new information technologies radically change the way goods and services are delivered. This New Economy paradigm has been more accurately termed by DeLong as the **Real-Time Economy**.[**] Many companies have begun to recognize that SCM is the key to build competitive advantage of their products and services in the marketplace.

[**] A **Real-time economy** is an environment where all the transactions between business entities are in digital format, increasingly generated automatically, and completed in real-time (as they occur) without store and forward processing. [*Source*: Real-Time Economy Community, realtimeeconomy.net]

Components of information systems

People	Computer system	Data	Network

IT professionals' system administrator, programmers & end users i.e., the persons, who can use hardware and software for retrieving the desired information.			The network means communication media (Internet, intranet, extranet etc.)

Hardware — Software

The hardware means the physical components of the computers i.e., server or smart terminals	System SW Application SW Utility SW	The data is the raw fact, which may be in the form of database. The data may be alphanumeric, text, image, video, audio, and other forms.

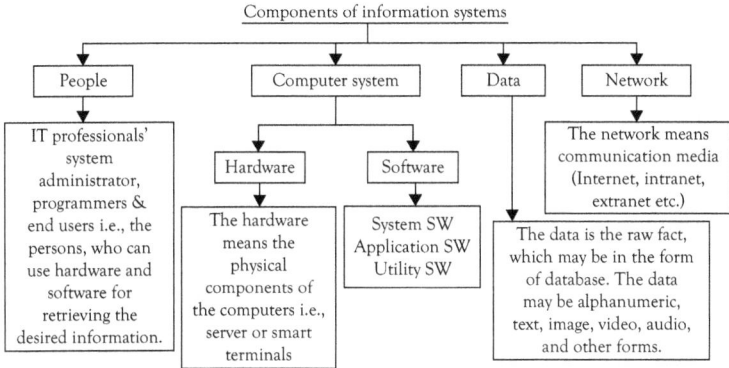

Figure 1.2 Components of information systems

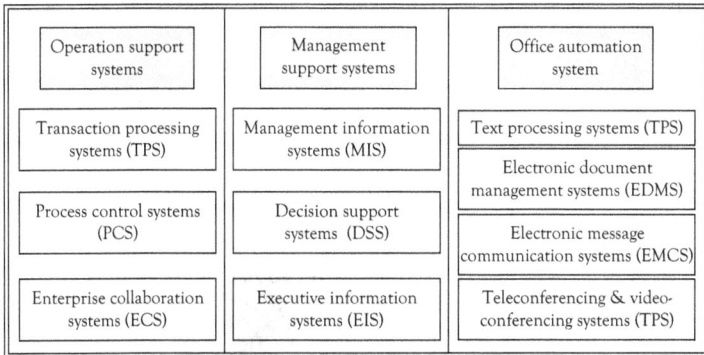

Operation support systems	Management support systems	Office automation system
Transaction processing systems (TPS)	Management information systems (MIS)	Text processing systems (TPS)
Process control systems (PCS)	Decision support systems (DSS)	Electronic document management systems (EDMS)
		Electronic message communication systems (EMCS)
Enterprise collaboration systems (ECS)	Executive information systems (EIS)	Teleconferencing & video-conferencing systems (TPS)

Figure 1.3 Types of information systems

In summary, supply chains contain a variety of channel activities such as purchasing and supplier management, third-party logistics, information exchange, marketing channels, demand planning, risk control, sales forecasting, and pricing strategies. Inside the chain, every member must present its unique operation in association with various SCM aspects to secure its future development and prosperity.

Notes

1. Smith (2006).
2. Drucker (2002, p. 196).
3. Adelaide (2003).
4. Stevenson and Hojati (2007, p. 587).
5. Lambert (2006, p. 2).

6. Tan, Lyman, and Wisner (2002).
7. McLeod and Schell (2000, p. 14).
8. Adapted from McLeod and Schell (2000).
9. DeLong and Summers (2001, pp. 29–59).

References

Adelaide, D. 2003. "World Socialists Web Site: Air Canada Using Bankruptcy Proceedings to Gut Jobs and Wages." http://wsws.org/articles/2003/apr2003/airc-a23.shtml

DeLong, B.J., and L.H. Summers. 2001."The New Economy: Background, Historical Perspective, Questions, and Speculations." *Economic review* 86, no. 4, pp. 29–59.

Drucker, P.F. 2002. *Managing in the Next Society, Part Three: The Changing World Economy, Chapter 12: The Global Economy and the Nation-state*, 196. New York, NY: St. Martin's Press.

Lambert, D.M. 2006. *Supply Chain Management—Processes, Partnerships, Performance: Chapter 1, Supply Chain Management: Introduction*, ed. D.M. Lambert, 2nd ed. Fisher College of Business, The Ohio State University, Supply Chain Management Institute, Sarasota, Florida.

McLeod, R., Jr., and G. Schell. 2000. *Management Information Systems: Part 1, Chapter 1: Introduction to the Computer-based Information System*, 14. Upper Saddle River, NJ: Pearson/Prentice Hall.

Smith, J.N. 2006. "World Trade Magazine: The Adam Smith of Supply Chain Management." http://worldtrademag-digital.com/worldtrademag/200609/?pg=70

Stevenson, W.J., and M. Hojati. 2007. *Operation Management: Chapter 16, SCM*, 587. 3rd ed. McGraw-Hill Ryerson Higher Education, Canadian edition.

Tan, K.C., S.B. Lyman, and J.D. Wisner. 2002. "SCM: A Strategic Perspective." *International Journal of Operations and Production Management* 22, no. 6.

CHAPTER 2

Needs and Benefits of Supply Chain Implementation

Introduction

In the current environment of a supply chain, companies are facing important challenges to establish their reputations on SCM implementation of their product lines and to re-engineer their values in the marketplace under competition.

For example, product merchandising is both an art and a science. The art involves the creation of a seamless connection of the physical experience to brand positioning.[1] These complex problems originate mainly from two drivers of change: people and technology. Major technological advances continue to evolve at an increasing rate. According to IBM, the buildout of the "Internet of Things" (IoT) will lead to the doubling of knowledge every 12 hours.*

For example, nanotechnology knowledge is doubling every two years; and clinical knowledge every 18 months. On average, human knowledge is doubling every 13 months.

These important changes in the world context present many business opportunities for entire industries. Companies in the supply chain have to take every chance to work on the issues of increasing efficiency, rebuilding structures, reducing costing, improving cycle time, and avoiding risks to catch up with contemporary market demands and fast-changing trends.

The tendency to innovative thinking, fast-changing competition, cost-driven and customer-based markets is very critical for any business.

---

* http://industrytap.com/knowledge-doubling-every-12-months-soon-to-be-every-12-hours/3950

Therefore, after businesses realize how to optimize various dimensions in working closer with their partners and customers by applying SCM properly, benefits such as quick response to market needs, higher customer satisfaction, lower inventory levels, effective communication among marketing channels, and fast delivery on a timely base can be easily achieved.

Just-in-time manufacturing also known as just-in-time production (**JIT**) is one of the most known examples of a method aimed at reducing flow times within production systems as well as response times from suppliers to customers. Its origin and development was in Japan, largely in the 1960s and 1970s and particularly at Toyota.[2] Alternative terms for JIT manufacturing have been used. Motorola's named this process short-cycle manufacturing (SCMfg),[3] whereas IBM used the term continuous-flow manufacturing (CFM),[4] and demand-flow manufacturing (DFM).[5]

The wide use of the term *JIT manufacturing* throughout the 1980s faded fast in the 1990s as the term *Lean Manufacturing*[†] became established as a more recent name for JIT.[6, 7]

Full Enhancement of the Purchasing Process

From the very beginning of applying SCM for the procurement of raw materials, companies must focus their purchasing management on a cost-oriented and supplier-sourced basis. Purchasing management in the supply chain discloses the contents and practices of business strategic advantages by optimizing the costing and pricing of finished products.

An SCM approach allows verifying one of the most effective processes for companies to preoccupy winning opportunities in advance. Using scenario-based decision making, companies are improving their purchasing workloads to more centralized operations, thus cutting redundant expenses such as costs of transportation, labor, opportunity, and training. The previous practices tend to improve supplier relationships and induce bulk purchases, which eventually can create imperative economies of scale to meet market demand and its pricing competitiveness. In comparison

---

[†] Lean manufacturing is a more recent name for JIT. As with JIT, lean manufacturing is deeply rooted in the automotive industry and focuses mostly on repetitive manufacturing situations.

with others, by implementing decentralized purchasing operations, the centralized operations require hiring smaller staffs, reduce transportation time, and increase product networking flexibility.

Business partners in the supply chain will observe the importance of coordinating purchasing activities among companies and try to fit in with a common strategy to assure purchasing operations will be implemented smoothly and successfully. To achieve quick response and higher efficiency, companies also need to open up their communication, negotiation, technology, innovation, and availability in purchasing processes to reach positive results and to share important benefits with every member of their supply chain.

Full Assurance of Quality Control

One of the greatest benefits of SCM is that companies not only manufacture higher quality products, but also recognize how to improve knowledgeably the quality function by using generic standards and better managerial operations. Important quality control challenges still exist in various industries. They include some fundamental issues such as:

1. Difficulties to establish, deliver, and market quality product to their customers successfully.
2. Difficulties to maximize quality in processing products and enhance their ability to compete.
3. Difficulties to reduce total costs existing in the chain and to retain simultaneously identical quality levels.
4. Difficulties to create more reliable operations in assuring complicated quality control procedures.
5. Difficulties to develop and maintain a competitive advantage on product quality.

Still, many quality control challenges exist that companies need to be concerned about and figure out solutions to them. Some of those challenges include mismanagement such as mistaken quality processes, misleading data exchanges, invalid system operations, and incompatible chain activities that can potentially lead companies to quality failure and affect product launch, market share, and company profitability.

However, these negative product quality events can be improved and reconstructed into a new business model once SCM is developed and applied. Right approaches to SCM are key factors leading to improvement of the quality functions resulting in higher company competitiveness. They drive companies to meet the high demand for qualified products and services by adopting integrated tools of advance technologies, build-to-order mass customization programs, vendor-managed inventory, and other innovative productivity initiatives. Applications on these latest systems and practices may affect many practical operations such as on-time scheduling and delivery, process cycle, cost reduction, inventory control, fill/return rates, and order lead times, which can be used effectively to improve and maintain the quality on their products.

Full Sourcing on Suppliers' Interdependence

Companies making intense efforts of supplier selection and interdependence build-up can achieve an important advantage in doing business globally. Such approaches can result in strong supplier partnerships, reliable sourcing, stable cost spending, solid technical supports, and more efficient operating processes.

Working out with proper suppliers is not only the art of getting the most out of these suppliers but also the strategies to hold them together as a team-based group to compete with their other counterparts, resulting in eventually benefiting companies to achieve their business goals such as maintaining brand equity, increasing chain efficiency, preventing lack of resources, lowering operating costs, improving qualitative productivity, and building long-term partnerships.

Discussion

Strategies to access suppliers' selection of partnerships or other business arrangements must be developed with some initial and ongoing assessment. They may include extensive business research, including surveys, certifications, and audits.

Sampling and statistical surveys can assist in better data collection techniques leading to sounder decision making. Other strategies such as surveys or polls, of course, can be conducted to find out supplier capabilities and their potential of closer collaboration in the same supply chain. Using a form of enterprise feedback management (**EFM**) throughout the supply chain can help an organization to establish a better dialogue with employees, partners, and customers regarding key issues and concerns, potentially resulting in making more effective customer-specific real-time interventions.[‡]

Certifications can establish a common language among various parties to identify an increased level of trust and understanding inside the chain. Certifications can also raise confidence for companies in keeping supplied products in diverse marketplaces and avoid shortages of reliable and sufficient supplies. Companies often certify suppliers at different levels to facilitate their needs for certain business requirements. Most of them will be based on suppliers' strength, weakness, opportunity, and threats: the **SWOT Analysis**.[§]

Audits provide third-party assurance to various stakeholders that the subject matter is free from material misstatement. The term is most frequently applied to audits of the financial information relating to a legal person. Other areas that are commonly audited include: secretarial & compliance audit, internal controls, quality management, project management, and energy conservation. As a result of an audit, stakeholders may competently evaluate and improve the effectiveness of risk management, control, and the governance process of the supply chain.

Early setup and development of strategic integration with suppliers can help drive the chain activities in harmonious, well organized, and streamlined processes, which will lead to important improvements in product competitiveness and availability in the marketplace. Results can be reached by bridging them with an extensive communication mechanism to open up the supply chain and to establish their mutual trust and cooperation on a solid relationship.

[‡] https://en.wikipedia.org/wiki/Enterprise_feedback_management

[§] A **SWOT analysis** is a strategic planning tool that helps a business owner to identify his or her own strengths and weaknesses, as well as any opportunities and threats that may exist in a specific business situation.

Rather than choosing one or two ways of working with suppliers, companies will need to adopt effective communication tools to spread and promote the exchange of market intelligence and data collection. Companies will also have to encourage constructive interactions with principle suppliers at all levels of their mutual activities to achieve high-performance operations when facing numerous competitors.

Cardinal Health Inc., for example, offers a comprehensive portfolio of supply chain services in the healthcare industry.* This company is one of the largest providers in the United States, with more than USD 130 billion in annual revenue projected in 2017.** By integrating its supply chain businesses, the company has leveraged significant resources to deliver solutions that can improve the operational performance of its customers and help make healthcare events more efficient. At the same time, by also standardizing its infrastructure and establishing best practices across its distribution network, Cardinal Health also increase its overall productivity. As a result of the changes by organizing around its core skills in distribution, logistics, procurement, finance, and information management into an effective supply chain, Cardinal expects to become more profitable as it serves a market that is about U.S.D. 300 billion (2016) in the United States alone.[8]

Notes

1. Arthur and Hemingway (2005).
2. Ohno (1988).
3. Heard (1987).
4. Bowers (March 1, 1991).
5. Roebuck (2011).
6. Black and Hunter (2003).
7. Hyer and Wemmerlov (2001).
8. Cardinal Integrates Supply Chain, Cardinal Health Inc. (October 10, 2005).

---

* http://cardinalhealth.com/en.html
** http://cardinalhealth.mediaroom.com/2017-08-02-Cardinal-Health-Reports-Q4-and-Fiscal-2017-Results-Provides-2018-Guidance

References

Arthur, R., and C. Hemingway. 2005. *Built for Growth: Expanding Your Business Around the Corner or Across the Globe.* 117. Upper Saddle River, New Jersey: Prentice Hall.

Black, J.T., and S.L. Hunter. 2003. *Lean Manufacturing Systems and Cell Design,* 41. Society of Manufacturing Engineers. ISBN: 9780872636477.

Bowers, G.H., Jr. March 1, 1991. "Continuous Flow Manufacturing." *Proc. SPIE1496, 10th Annual Symposium on Microlithography,* pp. 239–46.

Cardinal Integrates Supply Chain, Cardinal Health Inc. October 10, 2005. "New Unit for SCM." *Chain Drug Review* 27, no. 17, p. 21.

Heard, Ed. 1987. "Short Cycle Manufacturing: The Route to JIT." *Target* 2, no. 3 (fall), pp. 22–24.

Hyer, N., and U. Wemmerlov. 2001. *Reorganizing the Factory: Competing Through Cellular Manufacturing,* 41. Boca Raton, FL: CRC Press.

Ohno, T. 1988. *Toyota Production System: Beyond Large-Scale Production.* Boca Raton, FL: CRC Press.

Roebuck, K. 2011. *Business Process Modeling: High-impact Emerging Technology—What You Need to Know: Definitions, Adoptions, Impact, Benefits, Maturity, Vendors,* 32. Tebbo.

CHAPTER 3

Constitution and Network of a Supply Chain Organization

Introduction

SCM is essentially an efficient integration of labor, systems, facilities, and technologies, which affects suppliers, manufacturers, distributors, transporters, retailers, and final end-users when the materials are produced and distributed in a proper manner and in timely order. SCM also involves the coordination of key processes in a company such as order placement, order fulfillment, and purchasing, supported by marketing, finance, engineering, information systems, operations, and logistics.[1] Advanced technologies enable SCM to view the complete inflow and outflow of physical materials and the corresponding intangible information anywhere in the supply chain.

A good working state in the chain is a comprehensive well-organized sequence that starts from the customer's demand and ends at the supplier's raw material sourcing. Guidelines are applied to unify the product flow physically and information flow systematically up and down the whole supply chain in both directions and interchangeably. In many industries the supply chain is improved and optimized to achieve business goals such as removal of unnecessary costs, raise efficiency, refine logistic support, and smooth out operating processes.

Critical SCM elements involve three major components: its financial network (including for example, transportation cost information), its logistic network (comprising the relationship between the source of raw material and the retail distribution grid), and the physical transportation network (comprising for example, travel time information).[2]

The traditional path through the supply chain is from the **supplier** to the **manufacturer** through the **distributor** past the **retailer** to the **consumer**.

We review each of these supply chain entities' roles hereafter.

Role of Suppliers

A supplier in the supply chain can be any organization that has enough products or services flowing inside the chain before reaching the final end-user or customer. Generally, providers of raw materials are the original suppliers, positioned at the start the material flow in the supply chain. Furthermore, the supplier needs to provide the proper information along with the associated product requirements.

For example, furniture industries rely on forestry whereas heavy industries rely on oil.

Role of Manufacturers

Manufacturers are seen as key players in the supply chain. In general, manufacturers have their own suppliers who provide them directly with their required raw material from various sources.

The status of a manufacturing entity is based on how it manufactures product derived from a sourcing company and how it resells the product under its brand name. Regardless of manufacturers' types in a supply chain, they will focus on technical trends, innovative development, excellent performance, and associated market research. They will execute everything they can to keep their products in tune with the market requirements such as fashion, practice, affordability, and durability.

Companies that are positioned as manufacturing partners might be original equipment manufacturers (**OEM**),* original design manufacturers (**ODM**),† or original brand manufacturers (**OBM**).‡

---

* **OEM** (pronounced as separate letters) is short for **original equipment manufacturer**, which is a somewhat misleading term used to describe a company that has a special relationship with computer and IT producers. **OEMs** are manufacturers who resell another company's product under their name and branding.

† An **original design manufacturer** (**ODM**) is a company that designs and manufactures a product as specified and eventually rebranded by another firm for sale.

‡ An **original brand manufacturer** (**OBM**) is typically a company that sells an entire product made by a second company or including a component from a second company sources as its branded product. Selling the product of the second company under its brand just adds a virtual extrinsic value to the product.

Often, manufacturers are less prone at direct sales, which results from their unfamiliarity or range of their target markets. Few manufacturers may know how to find direct ways to sell their manufacturing products successfully at a point of sale and to save some costs by not going through warehousing or distribution. However, they still have to get involved to a certain extent with various partners inside the supply chain.

Role of Distributors

Distributors are also part of the providers' service logistics because of their involvement in transportation, wholesale, warehousing, shipping, assembling, and packaging. The finished goods, after leaving the manufacturers, will be delivered to their final points of sale located in different parts of the supply chain.

Distributors in the chain must go beyond offering warehouse services and accept orders or just forward material shipping. They usually play an important role as bridges connecting various entities of the supply chain. They are providing services, which normally include timely access to products, adding some administrative services for those products, and furnishing some level of information exchange support.

Role of Retailers

Retailers are typically the last link of the supply chain to the end-user. Because they work directly with the end-users, they are often regarded as the manufacturers' representatives and have firsthand information of product-related issues.

Retailers' changeable role often includes that of a sales agent, technical support, service consultancy, always balancing equal weight between manufacturers and customers. If more pressure was put on the manufacturer's side, retailers might lose customers by neglecting their rights. Pricing, for example, may affect both the manufacturers' profit margins, as well as customers' affordability. The goal to evenness is not that simple to reach for retailers. A critical cooperation must be maintained between manufacturers and customers: that of mutual respect and collaboration, based on knowledgeable management, to make products more competitive and more compelling for customers to purchase.

If retailers desire to figure out the best solutions inside the supply chain they must consider the key points that are contributing profitability simultaneously to manufacturers and satisfaction to customers. Otherwise, manufacturers may apprehend the role of retailers if their efforts and contributions are misunderstood.

Product Life Cycle

Lastly, the framework of a supply chain has a close relationship with the product life cycle, consisting of four stages—introduction, growth, maturity, and decline as displayed in Figure 3.1.

Based on the product's fundamental traits evolving from innovation to functionality, the supply chain must also change from a responsive approach to an efficient one.[3]

Companies in the supply chain have to deal with a high level of uncertainty because of market reactions to their products along with their life cycle. As a result, a responsive supply chain must be flexible enough to accommodate diverse market demands and deal with high market uncertainty. An efficient supply must also be designed to cope with a relatively stable market environment affected by low uncertainty. Through the changing market demand, companies in the supply chain must also align their strategies and organizations to the **product life cycle** evolution over time.[4] Otherwise, they may lower their business competitiveness, or even lose their market share.

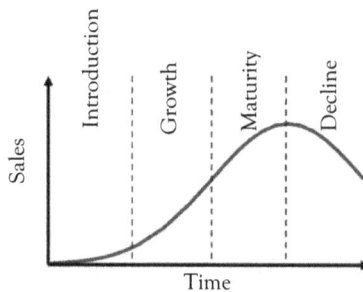

Figure 3.1 *The four stages of product life cycle*

Notes

1. Krajewski and Ritzman (2002, p. 498).
2. Coughlan et al. (2001).
3. Fisher (1997, pp. 105–17).
4. Bowon (2005, p. 182–85).

References

Bowon, K. 2005. *Mastering Business in Asia, SCM: Chapter 4, Strategic Management of a Supply Chain*, 182–85. Hoboken, New Jersey: John Wiley & Sons.

Coughlan, A.T., E. Anderson, L.W. Stern, and A.I. El-Ansary. 2001. *Marketing Channel, Chapter 16: Logistics and Supply Chain*. Routledge, UK: Abingdon-on-thames.

Fisher, M.L. March-April, 1997. "What Is the Right Supply Chain for Your Product?" *Harvard Business Review* 75, no. 2, pp. 105–17.

Krajewski, L.J., and L.P. Ritzman. 2002. *Operations Management: Strategy and Analysis, Part 5, Chapter 11: SCM*, 498. London, UK: Pearson Education.

CHAPTER 4

Innovation and Technology in Supply Chain Operations

Introduction

In the early 1990s, after information technology started to be applied more readily to business using the Internet, companies and their stakeholders could more easily communicate between themselves and develop online services on a global scale. The traditional model of business and society was shifting to a point where regional limits and time differences were no more important hurdles. The advent of the Internet as a business tool has seriously influenced the business setting on a microeconomic and macroeconomic basis, including trade relationships, natural resources, and environmental protection.

Throughout SCM applications, innovations and technologies have brought contributions in many respects by improving industrial efficiency and promoting economic prosperity. The SCM system has contributed to reducing production costs and redundant spending, stabilizing commodity volatility, strengthening resource recycling, and enhancing human welfare.

SCM and the Traditional Business Models

In the traditional businesses models, many productivity-oriented industries are focusing on product design and manufacturing skills rather than on process redesigning and manufacture re-engineering of their supply chain. Many issues, from moving raw materials, assembling components, to manufacturing products inside the supply chain can comprise a significant part of their total cost, timing, and labor after their products are launched. Therefore, applying SCM to their mode of operation can help improve their business planning, execution, supervision, review, and project audits.

SCM, Innovation, and Technology

Innovation and technology have also changed the business setting from narrow-minded localization to opened-up globalization. The more competition the business is facing, the more progress the business is making. When companies learn how to cooperate with their partners they realize how to better compete against their rivals.

Under this tendency, many nations have reached consensus or agreement through, for example, the World Trade Organization (**WTO**),* the North American Free Trade Agreement (**NAFTA**),† or the Asian-Pacific Economic Cooperation regional economic forum (**APEC**),‡ by removing trade barriers and encouraging a free world market, despite the tendency of the United States to abandon the free market under President Trump.§ As a result, SCM is expanding worldwide and connecting systematically companies, customers, marketplaces, services, and materials by formalizing innovations and technologies inside the chain. This important change is a significant shift in the delivery of products and services.

Companies in the supply chain must face changing business practices and adapt themselves to this new competition paradigm. SCM systems are becoming decreasingly expensive, less complicated, more accurate, and highly efficient.

In the United States, for example, better SCM appears to influence positively macroeconomic productivity and output. In addition to other factors, important changes and emerging trends in management practices have made companies more efficient. Furthermore, these changes, in turn, have ushered a more competitive business environment and contributed to the nation's improved macroeconomic performance.[1] The

---

* The World Trade Organization (https://wto.org/)
† The North American Free Trade Agreement (http://naftanow.org/)
‡ The Asia-Pacific Economic Cooperation (https://apec.org/)
§ http://newsweek.com/trump-abandoning-free-market-528579

effect of innovation and technology on the supply chain operations is important particularly in conjunction with increasing globalization.

Consequences Resulting from Innovation and Technology

To understand the consequences resulting from innovation and technology, companies need to adapt their business mission and purpose accordingly. To optimize the practices in the supply chain, companies need to primarily know their customers' requirements and seek strategies to satisfy their needs and desires.

Many sales data including customers' preferences, tastes, and styles are very useful to upstream manufacturers after they share the market information from other downstream supply chain partners, a tendency that has been very successfully implemented by a number of firms with major online presence, like for example[5]:

- Zappos, a leader in online shoe commerce. (www.zappos.com)
- American Express (AMEX) through its Open Forum website. (www.americanexpress.com)
- Mint, a finance management application (before its acquisition by Intuit). (www.mint.com)
- Uber, offering a form or "private" driver service. (www.uber.com)
- Dollar Shave Club, self-descriptive title. (www.dollarshaveclub.com)
- The Wirecutter, a product review website (acquired by the New York Times Company in 2016). (www.thewirecutter.com)
- Slack, a collaboration tool that allows teams to communicate more efficiently and share file. (www.slack.com)
- Airbnb, an online travel accommodation service. (www.airbnb.com))
- JetBlue, a discount airline website. (www.jetblue.com)

---

[5] For more information visit: https://singlegrain.com/digital-marketing/10-companies-doing-online-marketing-right/

- Yelp, combining social media and online reviews. (www.yelp. com)

Of course, companies such as Amazon, or eBay with major online presence, have also an impact of the online business model others pursue.

Moreover, for a company to establish long-term competitiveness, issues regarding distribution, warehousing, information exchange, and shipping can be integrated by using appropriate innovations and technologies such as electronic data interchange (**EDI**),** just-in-time manufacturing (**JIT**),†† material requirements planning (**MRP**),‡‡ vendor-managed inventory (**VMI**),§§ enterprise resource planning (**ERP**),¶¶

** **Electronic data interchange** (EDI) is an electronic communication method that provides standards for exchanging data via any electronic means. (https://en.wikipedia.org/wiki/Electronic_data_interchange)

†† **Just-in-time** (**JIT**) **manufacturing**, also known as **just-in-time production** or the Toyota Production System (TPS), is a methodology aimed primarily at reducing flow times within production system as well as response times from suppliers and to customers. Its origin and development was in Japan, largely in the 1960s and 1970s and particularly at Toyota. (https://en.wikipedia.org/wiki/Just-in-time_manufacturing)

‡‡ **Material requirements planning** (**MRP**) is a production planning, scheduling, and inventory control system used to manage manufacturing processes. Most MRP systems are software-based, but it is possible to conduct MRP by hand as well. (https://en.wikipedia.org/wiki/Material_requirements_planning)

§§ **Vendor-managed inventory** (**VMI**) is a family of business models in which the buyer of a product provides certain information to a supplier (vendor) of that product and the supplier takes full responsibility for maintaining an agreed inventory of the material, usually at the buyer's consumption location (usually a store). A third-party logistics provider can also be involved to make sure that the buyer has the required level of inventory by adjusting the demand and supply gaps.(https://en.wikipedia.org/wiki/Vendor-managed_inventory)

¶¶ **Enterprise resource planning** (**ERP**) is the integrated management of core business processes, often in real-time and mediated by software and technology. These business activities can include: product planning, purchase, production planning, manufacturing or service delivery, marketing and sales, materials management, inventory management, shipping and payment, and finance. (https://en.wikipedia.org/wiki/Enterprise_resource_planning)

efficient consumer response (**ECR**),*** collaborative planning, forecasting, and replenishment (**CPFR**),††† and radio-frequency identification (**RFID**),‡‡‡ to enable more efficient operations and practices.

Finally, the activities in the supply chain can be easily transformed into a distinct business model by applying innovation and technology. The efficient implementation of these new approaches drives companies to collect faster valuable customer data and analyze it in detail providing quick response throughout the supply chain.

In summary, information flow within businesses can be reorganized by using relevant technologies, resulting in better and timelier business decision making across all channels of the supply chain.[2]

*** **Efficient consumer response** (**ECR**) is a joint trade and industry body working toward making the grocery sector as a whole more responsive to consumer demand and promotes the removal of unnecessary costs from the supply chain. There are four focus areas under ECR: demand management, supply management, enablers and integrators, which are intended to be addressed as an integrated set. These form the basis of the ECR Global Scorecard. (https://en.wikipedia.org/wiki/Efficient_Consumer_Response)

††† **Collaborative planning, forecasting, and replenishment** (**CPFR**), a trademark of GS1 US, is a concept that aims to enhance supply chain integration by supporting and assisting joint practices. CPFR seeks cooperative management of inventory through joint visibility and replenishment of products throughout the supply chain. Information shared between suppliers and retailers aids in planning and satisfying customer demands through a supportive system of shared information. This allows for continuous updating of inventory and upcoming requirements, making the end-to-end supply chain process more efficient. Efficiency is created through the decrease expenditures for merchandising, inventory, logistics, and transportation across all trading partners. (https://en.wikipedia.org/wiki/Collaborative_planning,_forecasting,_and_replenishment)

‡‡‡ **Radio-frequency identification** (**RFID**) uses electromagnetic fields to automatically identify and track tags attached to objects. The tags contain electronically stored information. Passive tags collect energy from a nearby RFID reader's interrogating radio waves. Active tags have a local power source such as a battery and may operate hundreds of meters from the RFID reader. Unlike a barcode, the tag need not be within the line of sight of the reader, so it may be embedded in the tracked object. RFID is one method for automatic identification and data capture (AIDC). (https://en.wikipedia.org/wiki/Radio-frequency_identification)

Notes

1. Siems (2005).
2. Lee and Whang (2001).

References

Lee, H.L., and S. Whang. 2001. *E-business and Supply Chain Integration.* Stanford Global SCM Forum.

Siems, T.F. 2005. "SCM: The Science of Better, Faster, Cheaper." *Southwest Economy* 2, March/April, http://dallasfed.org/research/swe/2005/swe0502b.html

CHAPTER 5

Technical Analysis of SCM Systems

Introduction

In this chapter, we analyze various SCM technical characteristics and explore some of its related challenges. We examine some strategic development issues and practical problems associated with SCM implementation.

Risks and uncertainties may be followed by problems appearing to be threats to business growth if no proper solutions are found. Therefore, one needs to examine in more detail issues related to e-business, e-commerce, e-banking, e-auction, and e-learning in conjunction with SCM systems. More detail on this approach is presented to demonstrate how SCMs can assist companies in achieving e-business excellence.

SCM Challenges and Difficulties

Some international companies such as Toyota, Acer, Sony, Wal-Mart, and Samsung, for example, have deployed their unique SCM business strategies to establish best practice leadership over their competitors. By taking advantage of their approaches, these companies have achieved significant profitability in their respective markets and have benefited from their efforts by managing their supply chain efficiently such as sourcing raw materials, manufacturing products, procuring facilities, and distributing goods.

Businesses need to keep in mind that SCMs include diverse issues such as: efficient operational management, fast information networking, comprehensive system design, advanced management solution, and precise market forecasting. All chain activities must be preceded by solid teamwork with different chain partners including suppliers, manufacturers, distributors, wholesalers, shippers, retailers, and customers.

As business settings have become increasingly complex, adequate skills and expertise to manage the supply chain are required. Those requirements need to focus on SCM-related issues such as sourcing, manufacturing, warehousing, procurement, distribution, transportation, information, and the customer. Therefore, many companies have started to initiate supply chain integration to respond to their competitive challenges by using appropriate SCM-based technologies. However, people and relationships are the dominant issues of the day.*

Based on these concerns, companies are also keen to build supply chain partnerships and integrate all the supply chain elements for the benefits of every supply chain partner. They encourage close relationships by collaborating inside the supply chain and removing barriers affecting chain performance. When a supply chain is highly efficient, it can give chain members a powerful competitive advantage. However, when a supply chain is not working well, it can seriously influence the business' competitiveness and bottom line.

Companies have found that it is very challenging for them to identify problems in advance and relieve SC bottlenecks as needed. One of the challenges is how to handle the flow of goods and services and simultaneously coordinate those with the associated information and capital flow. Another difficulty is how to set up and implement business strategies to strengthen strategic advantage and to establish long-lasting competitiveness of their supply chain. Some of the critical SCM issues are related to changing distribution, addressing customer satisfaction, and removing bottlenecks. We cover those hereafter.

Difficulties in Changing Distribution Channels

During the process of distributing finished goods, a transformation from delivery by a traditional transportation company to a comprehensive multiservices company is becoming a trend. Reducing time and distance used for goods delivery results in savings, which can be translated into profits if the operation could be maximized by the adoption of advanced

---

* Supply Chain Challenges: Building Relationships, Harvard Business Review on SCM, p. 65.

technologies such as efficient shipment planning and inventory control, both by the shipper and the carrier.

Although distribution-related activities were once the lower expense part of the whole supply chain, they became more costly; this in turn may lead to a negative rethinking of the supply chain by giving the distribution function a less prominent role in the supply chain network. In light of this dilemma, companies in the supply chain had to re-evaluate their sourcing of raw materials, manufacturers, distributors, retailers, and consequently their whole supply chain.

In the early 1980s, for example, numerous companies in Taiwan have moved their roots to Mainland China to accelerate their distribution and reach their market more timely, particularly in the Asia-Pacific area. The speed to market was greatly improved, but the cost associated with the speed could also raise above the upper-limit of what companies can tolerate comfortably.

Customer Satisfaction Difficulties

Sometimes it is not practical trying to provide comprehensive services and expectations addressing every customer requirement. Customer satisfaction is a balancing act in the supply chain, where a constant tension exists among the chain members, such as, on one hand, customers' expectation of product quality, and on the another, suppliers' cost-cutting constraints. These requirements result in trade-offs or conflicts. Resolving those opposing issues represent substantial challenges to SCM members.

Solutions to the preceding challenges include a critical balancing act between commitments to customer expectations and to those of the chain members. Indeed, while customers are asking for service, quality, performance, functionality, price, and convenience, companies need to keep their products and services flowing efficiently in both directions from the supplier to the end-user, and vice versa to satisfy these customer needs. Furthermore, to meet customer expectations, companies have to maintain a constant level of secured inventory resulting in extra cost, to ensure fully that the products and services are timely available to their customers.

With a longer and more comprehensive supply chain, additional challenges may involve extended lead times, faster delivery, larger warehousing space, higher labor costs, and more expensive system upgrades to meet safety stock requirements. The contributions to customer satisfaction are part of the price to pay to win and maintain market share.

Difficulties in Bottleneck Removal

As activities take place throughout the supply chain, products and services delivered might result in more time-consuming, higher resource usage, and lower cost reduction than anticipated. To improve supply chain performance, companies must cooperate efficiently with their partners inside their supply chain. Nevertheless, in reality, it is very hard for every member of the supply chain to contribute advantageously to supply chain activities without a selfish mindset. Members of the supply chain usually invest considerable effort and hard work to benefit other supply chain members by using appropriate systems, processes, facilities, strategies, and approaches. The energy involved represents a long-term investment for chain members to keep their commitment to their partnerships without negatively affecting their profitability.

Some companies are always exploring ways that can best benefit them, which is, albeit, a short-sighted view, rather than searching for ways that could benefit the whole supply chain, a more far-sighted vision. Some-times, every member in a supply chain may easily achieve short-term profits, affecting later the long-term profits of the entire supply chain. How to reconfigure the entire chain and to develop a more effective strategy for each of chain member is often unclear because many elements can undermine a supply chain operation.

For example, China has developed an approach to SCM, which guarantees that most of the items in its supply chain will be shipped within 24 hours from Shanghai to any city in the United States. The key point was not the *speed* of moving items from their origin to their destination by a fast-designed supply chain mover, which can easily bypass the tedious processes of unnecessary intermediaries, but to *solve problems* relating to how well companies will learn to master the entire supply chain and how well they will figure out ways to remove every bottleneck across the supply chain to satisfy the requirements of the supply chain.

CHAPTER 6

Strategic Issues in Supply Chain Practices

Introduction

In this section, we discuss SCM's strategic issues and summarize them in three categories: complete data collection and accurate information exchange, efficient enhancements on visibility and resources sharing, and technological development and application.

Supply Chain Practices

The latest evolution in SCM includes supplier partnership, outsourcing, cycle time compression, continuous process flow, and information technology sharing.[1] Many approaches focusing on procurement, manufacturing, quality assurance, delivery speed, customer service, and facility management have been applied to SCM. Issues of operation integration, information exchange, process design, customer services, demographic analysis, and productivity enhancement must be addressed to help achieve the goals and objectives of ultimate supply chain superiority and maximize business competitiveness and its core competencies.

Four strategic elements consisting of strategic supplier partnership, customer relationship, level and quality of information sharing, and strategic operation procedures are often selected to measure supply chain practices, and review and verify the supply chain results. They cover mainly the upstream (strategic supplier partnership) and the downstream (customer relationship) sides of a supply chain, including information flow across a supply chain (level and quality of information sharing), and the internal supply chain processes (strategic operation procedures) as well as complete data collection, and accurate information exchange.

In some current supply chains, companies at different levels have loaded various data associated with products, processes, and services in certified data pools and exchanged them with their chain partners. Although the amount of useful data collection may not be available everywhere, a significant number of chain members understand the value of data collection to maximize their collaboration efforts.

For example, companies increasing their data collection by forecasting market demand* can improve their assessment and accuracy of the procurement of raw materials, which may result in increasing the capability and efficiency of manufacturing products to a secured inventory level.

Logility (see footnote 1), suggests that for:

Typically, a variety of forecasting methods are applicable to any particular supply chain scenario. Smart supply chain planners use multiple forecasting methods tuned to perform well at different phases of the product life cycle, chosen to best exploit the available historical data and degree of market knowledge. The key is to pick the most effective and flexible forecasting models, blend their best features, and shift between them as needed to keep forecast accuracy at its peak. [Ibid]

Therefore, the flow of products and services can be activated more reliably and faster to the customer side instead of slowed down by trade activities in data correction or updates at various points. The costs on inbound and outbound expenditures of the supply chain will be diminished. Complete data collections and accurate information exchange can increase business intelligence on market trends and provide more flexible operations on industrial movements in the supply chain. Not only can products and services move faster, but information also has an extensive application within the chain. Data collection and information exchange have become strategic issues, which might be significant factors for business development and growth.

---

* See "Eight methods that improve Forecasting Accuracy." https://logility.com/library/white-papers/demand-planning-papers/media/8-methods-that-improve-forecasting-accuracy

For example, in China, many retailers are providing inaccurate first-hand market reaction information to their chain partners from their numerous points of sale because of deficient know-hows and weakness in analytical skills. If companies, such as suppliers or manufacturers, cannot receive accurate and constant data to adjust their operations, the results derived from this information gap might negatively affect their decision-making process. Therefore, some companies have continuously emphasized the importance of improving their data collection and information exchange capability.

The keys to managing well the supply chain and maintain a strategic advantage are reliability and accuracy of available information.

SCM Benefits

Visibility enlargement and resource sharing in the supply chain present significant benefits by not merely providing information about the location and status of each shipment, but also by collaborating with their scattered resources to operate efficiently in achieving their business goals. They are the energy reinforcements of the entire supply chain.

Companies' abilities to quick response by using just-in-time systems, inventory controls (by adopting distribution requirements planning systems), and resource integration (by deploying enterprise resources planning systems) could remove easier the extra costs out of the supply chain and increase their core competencies. If companies could manage each step in the supply chain tightly, the risks and uncertainties associated with the chain activities would be minimized.

Enhancements on product visibility and resource sharing are the key to making any supply chain practice work well. In a typical supply chain, enhancing the product shipment visibility or handling from the point of departure to the point of destination are issues most associated with transportation. During this lengthy and complicated process, the information accompanying the shipment must be shared with every chain member to collaborate smoothly during the team-based activity.

For example, retailers in Taiwan can track shipments during the many stages involved. A company, as a third-party logistic provider in Hong Kong, can quickly follow the shipment and trace it back further up to the original manufacturer in China. This process is working well because each company involved in the supply chain has a hand in tracking the shipment and offers information visibility by sharing its mutual data resources. Therefore, the efforts to encourage companies willing to share their data resources and increase their visibility in the supply chain are imperative for a business to establish its long-lasting competitiveness.

Technological Development and Business Applications

Well-developed techniques have brought better applications to assist in managing the supply chain efficiently. Practices resulting from technological development and innovation to help the decision-making process are also becoming faster and cheaper. When new methods help companies design the SCM system and reduce the cost of operations, the results drive the supply chain more efficiently, and the companies inside the chain become more productive.

For example, Elizabeth Arden is a cosmetic manufacturer that markets and distributes to more than 100 companies its fragrances, cosmetics, and skin care products. It solved its logistic problem by using new technological solutions such as Precision Software's TRAXi3 system, enterprise resource planning system from JBA[†] residing originally on an IBM AS/400 computer to provide automated links with their partners. Since its acquisition by French Fragrances in 2001, Elizabeth Arden has increased its sales from U.S.D 382 million to nearly U.S.D 1 billion (2016). Annual earnings before interest, tax, and amortization (**EBITA**)[‡] have doubled to more than U.S.D 100 million. Elizabeth Arden's focus on logistics efficiency has allowed the company to achieve this level of international sales growth.[2]

[†] JBA was one of the world's leading business software providers in the 1980s and early1990s. Based in Birmingham, England, it had offices nationwide due to explosive growth partly because of the phenomenal success of IBM's "AS/400" midrange computer system. https://nicklitten.com/the-rise-and-fall-of-jba-soft-ware-as400-erp-system21/

[‡] Earnings before interest, taxes, and amortization (**EBITA**) refer to a company's earnings before the deduction of interest, taxes, and amortization expenses. It is a financial indicator used widely as a measure of efficiency and profitability.

In supply chain operations, industrial efficiency is also affected by new tools.[§] Technological improvements lower operation cost, production volatility, excessive inventory, lengthy process, and resources wasting.

For example, the 2001 recession resulting from major economic fluctuations and the 911 terrorist attacks set a record. However, consumer spending has remained relatively healthy despite these significant economic setbacks. Nearly every past recession was accompanied by a decline in consumer spending. However, in the first three quarters of 2001, consumer spending remained flat, but bounced back in the following two quarters, averaging a 3.8 percent annual growth rate. In other words, developing SCM expertise has shown a tremendous capability to overcome major business disruptions following a catastrophe, rousing customers' confidence that the economy will recover soon.[3]

Even though a recession may imply many negative bearings on economic development and supply chain performance, new technology solutions often bring up new answers. Therefore, no matter what factors affect production processes, information flow, inventory controls, delivery speed, and quality assurance, technological development and application always play a strategic role that profoundly engages SCM and fully ensures that businesses remain more knowledgeable and competitive.

Notes

1. Donlon (1996).
2. Foster (2007).
3. Ta-Win and Schmid (2002).

References

Donlon, J.P. 1996. "Maximizing Value in the Supply Chain—CE Roundtable—Panel Discussion, Chief Executive." http://findarticles.com/p/articles/mi_m4070/is_n117/ai_18926696

Foster, T.A. 2007. "Elizabeth Arden's Logistics Makeover More than Skin-deep, Global Logistics and Supply Chain Strategies." http://glscs.com/archives/04.06.arden.htm?adcode=15

[§] See: Thirteen Essential Supply Chain Management Tools at https://selecthub.com/supply-chain-management/13-essential-supply-chain-management-tools/

Ta-Win, L., and J. Schmid. 2002. "Economic Conditions During the 2001 Recession (Part I*), Washington Economic Trends, Research brief no. 15." http://ofm.wa.gov/researchbriefs/brief015.pdf

CHAPTER 7

Identifying Problems in Supply Chain Operations

Introduction

SCM is becoming more critical to figure out how to improve the core advantages and to increase the strategic competitiveness. In a supply chain, ideas to improve the process product delivery from its origin to its destination seem natural. If in practice this were that simple, there would be no need for specialized tools like those of a supply chain to figure out better delivery solutions. The common goal of any SCM is trying to increase business profit. Hence, for this to happen, the first challenge resides in developing a well-organized supply chain. To be considered efficient, the supply chain must be aligned to ensure that what the manufacturer produces meets customer demand and vice versa, what consumers want responds to the manufacturer's production. Often too many chain members are not aligned to collaborate harmoniously with each other. Some chain members are frequently functioning independently focusing on their benefit rather on the benefit of the whole supply chain. Then, useful information for the entire supply chain might be lost or misused.

Inventory Management in a Supply Chain

Inventory management strategy, for example, is a sensitive issue for supply chain members. Nobody is willing to be the first one to reach product stock-out in peak market demand resulting in lost customers. In those chains reactions, a business customer like a retailer may ask for the intermediary such as a wholesaler, responsible for warehousing, distributing, logistics, and packing to ensure that sufficient product is maintained in inventory. The intermediary may forward the request and ask the manufacturer to produce more safety stock; this inventory increase process will eventually move up to the original supplier for more raw materials inventory stocking, resulting in excessively high inventory levels as chain members get further from the end-customer, occasioning the *bullwhip effect,** which means that "the demand variability is progressively larger moving backward through a supply chain."[1] The bullwhip effect is a wasteful condition that occurs because of a lack of information-sharing across the supply chain. One cause for this can be that information varies with orders, sales, promotions, policies, processes, and systems all along the supply chain. The bullwhip effect can plague companies trying to make their supply chain more efficient by doing as best as they can to eliminate excess practices and tedious operations.[2]

Less Customer-Oriented Services

Other problems, besides the bullwhip effect, resulting in serious production inefficiency and information distortions throughout the supply chain, have also been identified.

For example, when products are sold to customers, every company in a supply chain related to the sold product does not end its service at that stage. Customers may end up having positive or negative reactions about the product they purchased. If the reactions are positive, they may intend to buy another product associating them with the same retailer or same manufacturer inside the same supply chain. On the contrary, if they respond negatively, customers will criticize the inferior product and forward their complaints to the same members of the associated supply chain.

---

* The **bullwhip effect** is a distribution channel phenomenon in which forecasts yield supply chain inefficiencies. It refers to increasing swings in inventory in response to shifts in customer demand as one moves further up the supply chain. The concept first appeared in Jay Forrester's *Industrial Dynamics* (1961) and thus it is also known as the **Forrester effect**. The bullwhip effect was named for the way the amplitude of a whip increases its length. The further from the originating signal, the greater the distortion of the wave pattern. In a similar manner, forecast accuracy decreases as one moves upstream along the supply chain. For example, many consumer goods have fairly consistent consumption at retail but this signal becomes more chaotic and unpredictable as the focus moves away from consumer purchasing behavior. Source: https://en.wikipedia.org/wiki/Bullwhip_effect

Many companies, such as in the automobile and computer industries, often realize their highest profits after they sell their original products. For these firms, customer service, warranty, postsale consulting, and technical supports have become critical parts of their revenues. Moreover, the growing requirements of complete customer-based services also engage companies in recycling products at the end of their life cycle, and improving environmental protection. These approaches drive SCM members to expand widely their understanding of customer satisfaction, another element that may affect their profitability.

Inaccurate Demand Forecast

When members in the supply chain place an order from either a manufacturer or a supplier, they need to consider capital sourcing, information exchange, and lead times calculation to replenish inventory to a safe level to meet market demand. However, different market requirements along with market fluctuations are very difficult to predict. Ensuing results may have negative bearings on the SCM and are likely to make chain operations hard to respond with proper actions.

Improper Delivery Costs Considerations

Because of higher fuel and labor costs, companies tend to place significant order volumes to save on repeated processing and transportation costs. Erratic orders on more shipments might trigger similar actions from both manufacturers and suppliers, which in turn may have an even more pronounced ripple effect throughout the supply chain, resulting in mitigating the savings on labor or transportation costs because more truckloads might be needed. Furthermore, warehousing costs, inventory, equipment, packing, quality control, and even brand equity may be higher than expected.

Inappropriate Pricing Strategy

Facing fierce competition, companies need to address unique product pricing strategies such as Wal-Mart's *Every Day Low Prices*, anniversary promotions, and price discounts to achieve profitability. This approach may cause customers to buy large product quantities and companies to stock large inventories.

Important market demand is activated to follow the special events on pricing strategy. When prices return to normal or the events do not match market demand, customers will stop buying. As a result, their buying pattern does not reflect their consumption pattern, which results in adverse effect on inventory levels, excessive production, and overestimated procurement that are difficult to handle by supply chain members.

Unavoidable Forces of Globalization

In many cases, SCM is unavoidably disintegrating smooth operations of the entire chain processes. For example, procurement, manufacturing, designing, packing, and marketing processes that were previously located in a same industrial zone are now spread out and controlled under different cultures, languages, and systems. These necessary changes in the supply chain have yielded many new problems such as unstable quality, unscheduled shipments, uncertain forecasting, complicated communications, financial mismanagement, and systemic dysfunction.

New supply chain operations improvements have triggered public debates on certain issues associated with supply chain complexity, which may lead to potential uncertainty risk. Issues of supply chain productivity may lead to possible complaints of price discrimination, or low-cost outsourcing that may lead to unexpected lay-offs.

Lack of Balance in Supply and Demand

According to **Keynesian Economics**,[†] a macroeconomic equilibrium will be reached after the market combines both the demand and supply sides

---

[†] "Keynesian economics" was used to refer to the concept that optimal economic performance could be achieved—and economic slumps prevented—by influencing aggregate demand through activist stabilization and economic intervention policies by government. Keynesian economics is considered to be a "demand-side" theory that focuses on changes in the economy over the short run. Ref: Keynesian Economics http://investopedia.com/terms/k/keynesianeconomics. asp#ixzz4u00n85YC

to determine a price level.[3] Keynesian Economics denotes that the concepts of price-leveling will be influenced by mutual forces of supply and demand.

If product demand in the marketplace exceeds supply, for example, a manufacturer may increase its production in pursuit of more profits. However, in turn, it may suffer if oversupply exists resulting in the price level suddenly dropping beyond expectation. Eventually, the orders from the market side will disappear, making it difficult for that manufacturer to forecast the real demand for its products.

Many companies in the supply chain have faced various problems regarding product demand and supply that changes significantly and unpredictably, forcing them to increase their manpower on production lines, hold excessive safety-level inventory, and speed-up product delivery. However, sizable market fluctuations make it very difficult for companies to manage processes, facilities, equipment, transportation, employees, capital, and information along their supply chain in a timely manner.

Lastly, even though the problems are unsettling supply chain operations, they can be solved by effectively applying SCM to reduce upstream variability in the supply chain, thereby improving operational efficiency, lowering costs, and increasing product quality. Moreover, downstream variability in the supply chain will also be diminished to meet market demand, stabilize profitability, and achieve customer satisfaction.

Notes

1. Stevenson and Hojati (2007).
2. Charles (2006).
3. Ragan and Lipsey (2005).

References

Charles, A. 2006. "Inventory Management Review: The Bullwhip Effect." http://Inventorymanagementreview.org/2006/05/the_bulwhip_eff.html

Ragan, C.T.S., and R.G. Lipsey. 2005. *Macroeconomics: Chapter 23, Output and Prices in the Short Run*, 573–83s, 11th ed. Pearson, Canada.

Stevenson, W.J., and M. Hojati. 2007. *Operation and Management, Third Canadian Edition: SCM: Challenges*, 603. Mcgraw-hill Ryerson.

CHAPTER 8

Risk Management in SCM Settings

Introduction

The importance of SCM as a comprehensive approach has increased tremendously since the 1980s.* SCMs have evolved from separate entities of suppliers, manufacturers, distributors, shippers, and retailers to integrated and well-organized mechanisms. Consistent with this evolution from logistics to supply chain practices, companies are remodeling their structures and re-engineering their frameworks to face and handle the full coverage of supply chain activities.

When their practices turn naturally to SCM systems, some companies are still focused on their individual performance and functionality rather than on the entire chain achievements. Therefore, more important configuration and a continuous SCM integration are needed. Integrated efforts from each member at all levels will help the whole supply chain develop a common set of **performance metrics** to achieve effective business operations.†

Supply chain performance refers to the extended supply chain's activities in meeting customer requirements, including product availability, on-time delivery, and all the necessary inventory and capacity in the supply chain to deliver that performance in a responsive manner. Supply chain performance crosses company boundaries since it includes basic

---

* https://i0.wp.com/cerasis.com/wp-content/uploads/2013/07/Supply-Chain-and-Logistics-Management1.png
† Supply Chain **Metrics** may include measurements for procurement, production, transportation, inventory, warehousing, material handling, packaging, and customer service. There are hundreds of **metrics** that can be used to score **Supply Chain Management** performance.

materials, components, subassemblies and finished products, and distribution through various channels to the end customer. It also crosses traditional functional organization lines such as procurement, manufacturing, distribution, marketing and sales, and research and development.

Performance measures, or "metrics," need to support global supply chain performance improvements rather than narrow company-specific or function-specific (silo) metrics, which inhibit chainwide improvements.

The SCOR Model for Supply Chain Strategic Decisions

The *supply chain operations reference model* (**SCOR**) is a management tool used to address, improve, and communicate supply chain management decisions within a company and with suppliers and customers of a company (1). The model describes the business processes required to satisfy a customer's demands. It also helps to explain the processes along the entire supply chain and provides a basis for how to improve those processes.[1]

The SCOR model was developed by the supply chain council[‡] with the assistance of 70 of the world's leading manufacturing companies. It has been described as the "most promising model for supply chain strategic decision making."[2] The model integrates business concepts of process re-engineering, benchmarking, and measurement into its framework. This framework focuses on five areas of the supply chain: plan, source, make, deliver, and return. These areas repeat along the supply chain. The supply chain council says that this process spans from "the supplier's supplier to the customer's customer."[3]

Plan

Demand and supply planning and management are included in the first step. Elements include balancing resources with requirements and determining communication along the entire chain. The plan also includes determining business rules to improve and measure supply chain efficiency. These business rules span inventory, transportation, assets, and

---

[‡] SCOR Model, Supply Chain Council, October 7, 2004. http://supply-chain. org

regulatory compliance, among others. The plan also aligns the supply chain plan with the financial plan of the company.

Source

This step describes sourcing infrastructure and material acquisition. It describes how to manage inventory, the supplier network, supplier agreements, and supplier performance. It discusses how to handle supplier payments and when to receive, verify, and transfer product.

Make

Manufacturing and production are the emphasis of this step responding to the questions of make-to-order, make-to-stock, or engineer-to-order. The make step includes production activities, packaging, staging product, and releasing. It also includes managing the production network, equipment and facilities, and transportation.

Deliver

Delivery includes order management, warehousing, and transportation. It also includes receiving orders from customers and invoicing them once product has been received. This step involves management of finished inventories, assets, transportation, product life cycles, and importing and exporting requirements.

Return

Companies must be prepared to handle the return of containers, packaging, or defective products. Returns involve business rules management, inventory return, assets, transportation, and regulatory requirements.

Benefits of Using the SCOR model

The SCOR process gives companies an idea of how advanced their supply chain is. The process helps companies understand how the five steps recur between suppliers, companies, and customers. Each step is a link in the supply chain that is critical in getting a product successfully along each level.

The SCOR model has proven to benefit companies that use it to identify supply chain problems. The model enables full leverage of capital investment, creation of a supply chain road map, alignment of business functions, and an average of two to six times return on investment.

This is just a brief overview of the SCOR model. It contains many more details and levels that can be analyzed within a company.[§]

Risk Distribution in SCM

A supply chain can work well only if the risks, costs, and rewards of doing business are distributed equitably across standard network metrics.[4] Standards developed by these metrics will help regulate the supply chain activities in an unbiased and just way.[5] The key to make sure that these processes can be done properly relies on interdependent coordination and collaboration of chain members, including suppliers, manufacturers, intermediaries, third-party service providers, and customers.

SCM Integration

In essence, SCM is a method of integrating various companies' supply and demand marketplace issues. SCM focuses mainly on removing functions by integrating them with those of the supply chain members. Companies can benefit from SCM tactics to coordinate easily with supply chain members and to facilitate efficient operation of complicated processes by using advanced technological tools and professional management solutions.

In a complex supply chain, anything can happen to entail various risks, which may include numerous issues from sourcing, manufacturing, distribution, all the way down to the customer. Companies often

---

[§] For more information, visit the Supply Chain Council website at www.supply-chain.org. A link to the SCOR model can be found on this page. A PowerPoint presentation that describes the entire SCOR process can also be downloaded.

encounter important risks with unexpected market demand spikes, raw material price fluctuations, longer shipment delays, natural disasters, sudden production lines breakdowns, strike disputes, financing difficulties, and instable socioeconomic unrests. Those events are impossible to be predicted accurately, but the probability that any of them will happen anytime is real.

Taiwan Example

For example, in 1999 Taiwan suffered a nationalwide power shutdown resulting from a large-scale natural disaster landslide. The Chi Mei Corporation, a Taiwanese plastic giant, which is also the world's largest manufacturer in producing AS resin,[*] lost about U.S.D 6 million in productivity that day. Through a ripple effect, the associated negative effect on the entire business was U.S.D 330 million.[6]

To reduce damages and enhance risk management, companies rely on sophisticated SCM systems and software because they realize that any supply chain disruption can destroy their production and affect their financial health. No matter what happens, earthquakes, transportation congestions, labor strikes, or bankruptcies, potential risks facing the marketplace are everywhere. The more the supply chain is working globally, the less the supply chain can buffer risk.

For example, many Taiwanese companies have their commanding headquarters in Taiwan handling the issues on capital sourcing, technical research and development, and human resources management. They build factories in China and import raw materials from South Asia. The finished goods are eventually delivered and sold in Europe and North America. From this business model, more activities such as sourcing, manufacturing, procurement, warehousing, inventory, and distribution are located in different countries and even on different continents. Business risks are likely to show up at any point and any moment, which means that companies running business globally have less capability relative to

---

[*] A copolymer of acrylonitrile and styrene used in food containers, water bottles, kitchenware, computer products, packaging material, battery cases, and plastic optical fibers.

the supply chain to mitigate those risks. Therefore, risk management becomes a strategic issue for any multinational company involved with a global supply chain. Enterprise risk management (**ERM**) is one of the most popular practices in place to help and enable companies to be more efficient in responding to business risk.[**]

The SCM Risk Management Process

The following procedures have been considered as proper processes regarding risk management demonstrating risk management focus.

Risk management includes:

1. Developing a risk backup plan that can be executed to ensure continued performance of the supply chain and maintain its essential operations, functions, flow, services, and capabilities as required.
2. Identifying risk and empowering employees at lower organization levels or implementing suitable arrangements of succession in leadership to establish authority under risky situations and ensure that decision making can be done during any emergency.
3. Preparing alternate personnel, organizations, and facilities for possible alternative operations in case of unexpected events.
4. Providing necessary programs for chain members in risk management training and exercising.
5. Verifying that all information and messages are available in backup databases to analyze critical risks in order of probability and effect on business and confirm their priority in risk models.

[**] Enterprise risk management (ERM) is a plan-based business strategy that aims to identify, assess, and prepare for any dangers, hazards, and other potentials for disaster—both physical and figurative—that may interfere with an organization's operations and objectives. Relatively new (it's less than a decade old), the discipline not only calls for corporations to identify all the risks they face and to decide which risks to manage actively; it also involves making that plan of action available to all stakeholders, shareholders, and potential investors, as part of their annual reports. Industries as varied as aviation, construction, public health, international development, energy, finance, and insurance all utilize ERM. Ref: https://investopedia.com/terms/e/enterprise-risk-management.asp

6. Establishing effective communication to comprehensive connectivity of entire supply chain members and their customers.
7. Investing in systems and software to efficiently control risks and manage them to sustain business operations.

Regardless of the business companies are in, the rules of risk-taking are the same. Companies have always responsibilities to ensure that their products and services meet customer satisfaction under any circumstance. Otherwise, some unmitigated risks can take companies out of business. Customers at all times will never care how companies suffer risk or ever forgive them for any excuse in that matter. They just switch their buying preferences to other companies and their respective products.

ERM is essentially a process imposed by an entity's board of directors, managers, and other personnel, applied in strategy settings and across the enterprise, designed to identify potential events that may affect the entity, and manage risk to be within its risk comfort zone, and provide reasonable assurance regarding the achievement of entity objectives.

Enterprise Risk Management Within SCM

ERM is embedded in the business environment. Risk management concerns process enhancement of the entire supply chain.

The ERM process will be affected by people at every level by applying appropriate strategies. SCM members need to understand the costs and losses associated with a variety of risks; and manage them simultaneously as products move from the source down to the customer within the supply chain. Risk management can preserve valuable resources and reduce business loss.

ERM provides useful mechanisms of risk forecasting and control; and presents opportunities for supply chain members on the issues of collaborative planning, systemic integration, and operational flexibility. To establish the ability of crisis control and to maintain sustainability, these approaches are imperative and necessary for companies facing unknown risks and uncertainties. To optimize ERM and to adapt it within an SCM in an integrated framework, companies must follow consistent performance metrics, share risk information, distribute secured resources, devote technological efforts, and build up mutual trust.

Any supply chain member's most significant concern is preventing, managing, controlling, mitigating, and even eliminating business risk wherever and whenever possible. The supply chain risk leadership council has published online a detailed handbook presenting a compilation of supply chain risk management best practices.[††]

Notes

1. Scott (2004).
2. Huan, Sheoran, and Wang (2004, pp. 23–29).
3. Supply Chain Operations Reference Model (October 7, 2004).
4. Committee of Sponsoring Organizations of the Treadway Commission (September 2004).
5. Norek and Isbell (October 2005).
6. Power Shutdowns: Important Loss (1999).

References

Committee of Sponsoring Organizations of the Treadway Commission. September 2004. "Enterprise Risk Management—Integrated Framework: Executive Summary." http://coso.org/Publications/ERM/COSO_ERM_ExecutiveSummary.pdf

Huan, S., S. Sheoran, and G. Wang. 2004. "A Research and Analysis of Supply Chain Operations Reference (SCOR) Model." *Supply Chain Management: An International Journal* 9, no. 1, pp. 23–29.

Supply Chain Operations Reference Model. October 7, 2004. Supply Chain Council.

Scott, H. October, 27, 2004. "The SCOR Model for Supply Chain Strategic Decisions." https://scm.ncsu.edu/scm-articles/article/the-scor-model-for-supply-chain-strategic-decisions

---

[††] Supply chain risk management: A compilation of best practices, (August 2011), http://scrlc.com/articles/Supply_Chain_Risk_Management_A_Compilation_of_Best_Practices_final[1].pdf

Norek, C.D., and M. Isbell. October 2005. "SCM Review, The Infrastructure Squeeze On Global Supply Chains: A Crisis is Brewing in the U.S. Transportation Infrastructure." *Supply Chain Management Review* 9, no. 7, p.18–24.

Power Shutdowns: Important Loss. 1999. *China Evening News*, July 30. http://gcaa.org.tw/env_news/199907/88073005.htms

CHAPTER 9

Correlation Between E-Business and E-Supply Chain

Background

The terms e-business and e-commerce are often used interchangeably. To differentiate those terms we propose the use the definition presented by the U.S. Government's Census Bureau as follows[1]:

E-Business Definition

E-business is any process that a business organization conducts over computer-mediated networks. Business organizations include any for-profit or nonprofit entity. Examples of major e-business process categories include: online purchasing, selling, production management, logistics, as well as internal communication and support services. Within each major category one can identify more specific processes. For example, online purchasing includes the following online processes: access to vendors' products/catalogs, ordering from vendors, electronic payment to vendors, vendor managed inventory, use of electronic marketplaces, and online auctions. Internal processes include: e-mail capabilities, automated employee services, training, information sharing, video conferencing, recruiting, and telecommuting.

E-Commerce Definition

Electronic commerce (e-commerce) is the value of goods and services sold over computer-mediated networks. An e-commerce transaction is "completed" when agreement is reached between the buyer and seller online to transfer the ownership or rights to use goods or services. This online agreement is the trigger for determining an e-commerce transaction, not the payment. Only priced transactions will be measured. Downloads of free software, for example, will not be measured. While transactions involve buyers and sellers, we generally will measure e-commerce from the seller's perspective. Examples of e-commerce transactions include the sale of a book or CD over the Internet, an electronic marketplace selling parts to another business, a manufacturing plant selling electronic components to another plant within the company using the company's Intranet, and a manufacturer selling to a retailer over an EDI network.

SCM and e-Commerce

When the UK's largest camera chain, Jessops, went under in 2013, the staff at one specific store posted a sign that was both sweet and sardonic: "Thank you to all our loyal customers and to everyone else, thank you for shopping at Amazon.com."[2]

The earlier event exemplifies how the advent of the Internet affected e-commerce. Whereas Internet has eased merchandising constraints by enabling retailers to sell to consumers anywhere in the world, still significant geographic constraints on the logistics and fulfillment of supply exist.[3]

Building fulfillment centers designed to cater to e-commerce, which demands the ability to handle a large number of small orders, can help retailers conduct more profitable online sales. Traditional warehouses are built to store pallets of products that are moved by forklifts to and from bays where trucks are loaded and unloaded. An e-commerce facility, on the other hand, is fine-tuned for individual items, more like a sorting facility for parcel handling, to be picked and packed for individual shoppers.

Even with distribution centers across vast regions, supply can nonetheless be restricted because of the costs that come with buying and holding inventory, not to mention building and maintaining these facilities.

Because of its important influence on business, e-commerce has grown quickly and expanded. This expansion has forced supply chain members to be more responsive to their customers. At the same time, competitive pressures induced cost-reduction and increase in operation efficiency. As a result, companies must work hard under competition to manage better the supply chain performance and focus on core strategies in the fast-changing marketplace to ensure that customer satisfaction needs are met. Increasing complexity and extensive commercial activities in a supply chain not only increases global competition but also severely aggravates business capabilities.

SCM Planning

The lengthy product journey from order planning to the end-user is filled with numerous pressures forcing every member in the supply chain to be aware of customer-oriented transactions as a top priority. However, only efforts focusing on planning customer needs are not enough for business development. The key is in how a supply chain can enhance the process to satisfy customers in a timely, convenient, efficient, and cost-saving manner.

Therefore, supply chain in most industries has to extend beyond traditional approaches to an e-supply chain, which includes planning and designing of website portal and order fulfillment. The former is a front-end window, which allows customers to order the products they desire. The latter is a back-end system, which involves order processing, manufacturing, warehousing, distributing, shipping, financing, delivering, and servicing.

To mitigate the earlier market challenges, APICS* Bolstorff suggests seven basic principles that the best planning organizations adopt[4]:

1. Systematic management of "master data," including key data fields for items, customers, manufacturing resources, and suppliers.
2. Synchronized long-term, tactical, and execution planning processes, planning horizons, and intervals for data refresh.
3. Mature collaborative processes for both key customers and suppliers reconciling forecast, orders, and usage or sell-through.
4. Data-oriented understanding of the inputs to the forecast including forecast error, cumulative bias, lift, new products, and year-end volume variation.

---

* APICS is the association for SCM at http://apics.org/apics

5. Intense focus on "point-of-sale" or "sell-through" data (as opposed to sales orders and "sell in").
6. Disciplined product lifecycle management process bridging the gap between product development and supply chain.
7. A continuous improvement approach to understanding consumer or user behavior.

During e-business practices, many problems regarding online activities are associated with networking issues in an e-supply chain. For example, when customers put an online order using the Internet, they expect that what they ordered can be delivered as soon as possible and precisely as it looked online. The ability to respond to orders quickly creates challenges every member in the supply chain needs to meet to satisfy customers' expectations. Quick ordering from customers also creates uncertainties and fluctuations on supply chain performance making it hard for companies to forecast market demand resulting in increased costs by having to maintain higher inventory.

SCM Billing

Another typical issue of online processes is billing. The entire online business typically requires Internet-enabled financial transactions throughout the supply chain. These financial operations must be linked together by the proper technology to create an integrated supply chain that provides trust, credit, authentication, visibility, authority, and legalization from the customer end up to each chain member. However, even though the technology can be customized for e-business applications, in practice, it is likely to contain some traps such as fraud or deceptions hurting the supply chain. Therefore, to better apply e-business in an e-supply chain one needs to address important challenge associated with these financial operations issues.

Before an e-supply chain structure is implemented, companies need to identify the causes that may affect an e-supply chain development. In addition to the previous examples, new problems on an e-supply chain can be attributed to some major categories such as lack of expertise in demand forecasting, insufficient information exchange, shortages of collaboration between chain members, improper process integration, ineffective framework deployment, and inefficient resource-sharing. Despite these limitations, e-business chain integration has been done successfully using innovative technological solutions. Indeed, companies such as **Oracle**,[†] **SAP**,[‡] and **i2Technologies**,[§] have developed many tools to help and provide technical support for e-supply chain functionality. These tools facilitate the handling of a large number of transactions, performing with a high degree of efficiency, having fully reliable functionality, rapidly capturing large volumes of data, accurately implementing extensive transaction evaluations, and comprehensively analyzing myriad information from greatly dispersed marketplaces worldwide. These e-business characteristics are also best applied on e-supply chains, which can sustain specific requirements of business developments and an increase in globalization.

Notes

1. Mesenbourgh (2001).
2. Jeremy (2013).
3. Kim (2015).
4. Bolstorff (2015).

References

Bolstorff, P.A. May 20, 2015. "The Seven Principles of Effective Supply Chain Planning." *Thinking Supply Chain, APICS.* http://apics.org/sites/apics-blog/think-supply-chain-landing-page/thinking-supply-chain/2015/05/20/the-seven-principles-of-effective-supply-chain-planning

---

[†] With 430,000 customers in 175 countries, **Oracle** provides leading-edge capabilities in software as a service, platform as a service, infrastructure as a service, and data as a service. https://oracle.com/index.html

[‡] **SAP** is the world leader in enterprise applications in terms of software and software-related service revenue. Based on market capitalization, we are the world's third largest independent software manufacturer. https://sap.com/corporate/en/company.html

[§] **i2Techonologies** [Innovative Information Technologies] is an innovative software company providing custom-made software for business application. http://i2technologies.net/about_us.php

Jeremy, H. August 2013. "Evolving the Supply Chain in the–e-Commerce Age." http://multichannelmerchant.com/must-reads/evolving-the-supply-chain-in-the-ecommerce-age/#_

Kim, N. May 7, 2015. "Wal-Mart Builds Supply Chain to Meet e-Commerce Demands." *The Wall Street Journal*, https://wsj.com/articles/wal-mart-builds-supply-chain-to-meet-e-commerce-demands-1431016708

Mesenbourgh, T.L. August 2001. *Measuring Electronic Business, U.S. Bureau of the Census*, 4. https://census.gov/content/dam/Census/library/working-papers/2001/econ/ebusasa.pdf

CHAPTER 10

SCM Operational Concerns Among Chain Members

Introduction

A supply chain can work well only if the risks, costs, and rewards of doing business are distributed fairly across the network's members. Metrics and Standards developed by supply chain members will help regulate the supply chain activities in a fair and just manner.[1] The key to ensure that SCM processes can be done efficiently relies on the interdependent coordination and collaboration within chain members. In essence, SCM is a method to integrate various companies on issues of supply and demand in the marketplace BY removing constraints to reach successful SCM business integration. Companies can benefit from SCM to easily coordinate supply chain members' operations and facilitate the operation of complicated processes by using advanced technology tools and professional management solutions. These can be achieved through effective supplier management and purchasing methods.

Supplier Management

Purchasing is the function of finding the best suppliers in the supply chain. Every company in the supply chain must know where it can buy the best products in a dispersed marketplace. To consider supplier selection and to check the supplier's performance, companies need to choose the products they want to sell, the customers they desire to serve, and relate these to the supply chain. Companies working in supply chain operations have developed a set of requirements and standards in choosing suppliers based on their competitive priorities.

For example, a construction company building houses uses quality control and on-time delivery as the top two factors for supplier selection. These factors reflect the primary considerations that the supply chain associated with the construction industry need to be concerned about. Suppliers have to link their capabilities and their market requirements. Notwithstanding these criteria, many suppliers are still incapable of communicating their messages about how excellent their products are. Little attention is paid to emphasize the selling content on *pricing, quality, performance, delivery,* and *service,* which are the five most important criteria to be considered when selecting suppliers because of the financial considerations involved. Indeed, the costs concealed everywhere along the supply chain will directly affect profitability.

When choosing suppliers, finding the best quality at the lowest price is always the key objective. The quality factor is critical to ensure product functionality, durability, and life expectancy. Quality assurance is also a reflection of how companies can demonstrate their product-launching ability. Poor quality damages not only reputation and goodwill but can also cause customer loss, especially loyal ones, which may result in profit loss.

Another performance consideration is associated with how the product meets customer needs, which means how much of customer expectations can be met when using the product. If the product does not meet customer expectations, it is likely to be returned for refund or exchange. The extra costs and customer discomforts will affect business as well.

On-time delivery is another factor in selecting suppliers; it helps companies shorten purchasing lead times and maintain lower inventory levels. A quick, reliable, and timely delivery can eliminate the uncertainties of product supply and improve cost control.

For example, daily demand in China for Toyota SUVs is typically distributed with a mean of 2,500 and a standard deviation of 500.[2]

A key component used in the car assembly is the powered steering wheel. The wheel suppliers take an average lead-time of seven days to replenish Toyota's inventory. Toyota is targeting a cycle service level

(**CSL**)* of 90 percent for its wheel inventory. If the standard deviation of the lead-time is also seven days, the safe inventory levels of steering wheels that Toyota must carry are calculated as follows:

Average demand per period, R = 2,500

Standard deviation of demand per period, σ_R = 500

Average lead time for replenishment, L = 7 days

Standard deviation of lead time, S_L = 7 days

Mean demand during lead time, $R_L = R \times L$ = 2,500 × 7 = 17,500

Standard deviation of demand during lead time,

$$\sigma_L = \sqrt{L\sigma_R^2 + R^2 S_L^2} = \sqrt{7 \times 500^2 + 2500^2 \times 7^2} = 17,500$$

The required safety inventory (SS) is obtained by:

SS = F^{-1}(CSL) × σ_L = NORMSINV (CSL) × σ_L = NORMSINV (0.9)
    × 17,550

    = 22,491 steering wheels.

See footnote: **NORMSINV**[†]

If the standard lead-time deviation is seven days, Toyota must carry a safety inventory of 22,491 wheels. This is equivalent to about nine days demand for steering wheels. However, if the lead-time was decreased from seven days to two days, the safety wheel inventory will be reduced to 2,2491 by using the same formula listed previously. The safety inventory will also decline from about nine days to less than two days.

Based on the aforementioned, lead time is one of the major factors that can seriously affect the inventory level, and subsequently increase or decrease inventory costs.

Finally, the supply chain activities must be the focus on customer-oriented concerns. Customer satisfaction is the supreme goal for any

---

* In supply chain the **cycle service level** (CSL) or just **service level,** is the expected probability of not hitting a stock-out during the next replenishment **cycle**, and thus, it is also the probability of not losing sales. The **cycle** duration is implicitly the lead time. https://lokad.com/service-level-definition

[†] **NORMSINV** is a Microsoft Excel function that delivers the inverse of the cumulative standardized normal distribution. When entering the "probability that a value Z is up to…" it returns that value Z (in terms of "sigma," because it is the standardized distribution with average 0 and sigma 1. https://isixsigma.com/dictionary/normsinv/

company expecting to run a business successfully. Companies cannot survive without considering their customers' needs as top priority.

Taking a closer look at Toyota again, this company represents a typical example of performing well its supply chain activities. Facing competition against other auto giants such as General Motors, Ford, and BMW, according to Bertel Schmitt (Forbes Magazine) as of January 2017, Toyota is set to remain the world's largest automaker (Schmitt 2017).

Back in the 1980s, Toyota invented Just-in-Time, which it called the "Toyota Production System," as one of the most popular systems focusing on cost reduction, quality assurance, performance achievement, on-time delivery, and customer service. This system has long been hailed as the source of Toyota's outstanding performance as an auto manufacturer.[3] Furthermore, back in the early 1990s, Toyota implemented a Lean Production system.[‡]

Despite that, many challenges still existed in the next few years. However, recent results show that Toyota's lean thinking has set the standards for this discipline. By applying its lean techniques on its supply chain, Toyota often created a significant competitive advantage that its other competitors had difficulty to copy. From the view of the customer, Toyota is no doubt the best supplier in providing a variety of vehicles at reasonable prices, excellent quality, superior performance, timely delivery, and satisfactory customer service.[4]

Toyota's Keiretsu[§] supplier network may have up to a 25 to 30 percent cost advantage relative to its peers.[5] Hence, when Toyota moved to the United States in the late 1980s, it insisted in establishing a similar supply chain network as the one it had in Japan.

[‡] **Lean manufacturing** or **lean production**, often simply "**lean**," is a systematic method for waste minimization ("Muda") within a **manufacturing system** without sacrificing productivity. **Lean** also takes into account waste created through overburden ("Muri") and waste created through unevenness in workloads ("Mura"). https://en.wikipedia.org/wiki/Lean_manufacturing

[§] A **keiretsu**, literally *system, series, grouping of enterprises, order of succession*) is a set of companies with interlocking business relationships and shareholdings. It is a type of informal business group. The *keiretsu* maintained dominance over the Japanese economy for the second half of the 20th century.

From the views of supplier management, Toyota has obviously influenced the U.S. auto business in a significant way by implementing small-lot, high-velocity supply chain practices. Toyota has developed a *demand-driven pull system*,⁵ which has been executed at all levels from physical distributions to information exchange and sales.

Raw materials, parts, and components in innovative packing and shipments can be quickly delivered to each node of a supply chain. Small-lot, high-velocity, instant orders, and on-time deliveries mean lower inventory level requirements, lower labor costs, and fast turnovers of finished-goods without affecting customer satisfaction. Toyota spreads out supplier management solutions and applications in its supply chain based on cost requirement, quality, performance, delivery, and service.

Over time, many companies in different industries perceived the differences and uniqueness of Toyota's approach. They noticed the importance of the purchasing process all the way to materials sourcing by using the "Toyota" criteria set in their supplier management system. They also learned to work efficiently across boundaries in a seamless manner; and to understand fully that their best interests are aligned with the best interests of the entire supply chain.

Effective Purchasing in the Supply Chain

Purchasing in the supply chain is defined as the management of the acquisition process, which includes deciding which suppliers to use, negotiating contracts, and deciding where to buy.[6]

---

⁵ A **pull system** is a lean manufacturing strategy used to reduce waste in the production process. In this type of **system**, components used in the manufacturing process are only replaced once they have been consumed so companies only make enough products to meet customer demand. A "**Push type system**" means "**make to stock**" meaning that production is not based on actual demand but on estimated or foreseeable demand. A "**Pull type system**" means "**make to order**," meaning that production is based on actual demand. In supply chain management, it is important to carry out processes halfway between push type and pull type or by a combination of push type and pull type. Ref: http://lean-manufacturing-japan.com/scm-terminology/push-pull-manufacturing.html

Purchasing is one of the key parts that can affect a supply chain's profitability and partnership cooperation. Successful SCM needs to integrate the entire activities for each of the chain members regarding planning, sourcing, manufacturing, purchasing, logistics, and customer service. Companies such as suppliers and manufacturers, for example, are bearing in mind their costs of finished goods resulting from the purchase of raw materials, parts, components, and equipment. Wholesalers and retailers have to purchase all goods first to initiate their business.

The importance of purchasing is also associated with product issues such as pricing, quality, timing, function, and delivery. These issues have a significant effect on supply chain performance. In practical business operations, purchasing plays the role of a bridge connecting each member in the supply chain. The primary goals of purchasing are not only to support business operation activities and form tighter partner relationship, but also help develop the requirements of physical distribution and sustain technical research on new products.

Many companies have transformed their traditional vertical purchasing integrations to horizontal ones shifting to the supply chain with their collaborative partners to achieve those goals. Effective practices on purchasing have been verified as follows[7]:

1. Buy items at the right price;
2. From the right source;
3. With the required specifications;
4. In the right quantity;
5. For delivery at the right time;
6. To the right customer.

Failing to satisfy these purchasing requirements may affect a company's long-term transaction benefits with suppliers who could eventually break the partner's relationship, which is hard to rebuild once lost.

As many companies tended to put more attention to marketing, more resources were allocated to product launching and market targeting rather than to purchasing practices. Results from this approach often frustrated the companies with lower profit margins even if sales and revenues increased after the product reached the marketplace successfully.

Therefore, the concept of focusing on marketing has gradually changed to focusing on purchasing. Given that factors such as multiple sourcing, cost reduction, operation efficiency, quality assurance, system performance, on-time delivery are strongly associated with purchasing issues, the best way for companies to improve profit is always from their starting point inside the supply chain. The more they can save by applying proper purchasing practices, the more they can use operational resources, and the more profit they can make from product sales. Profit resulting from purchasing is increasingly surpassing that from marketing applications.

Because of competition, companies in the supply chain encounter tremendous challenges and pressures in business development. Therefore, it is very critical to focus on effective purchasing management to reduce costs, reinforce partnerships, increase efficiency, stimulate innovations, improve quality, and simplify processes.

Achieving Effective Purchasing

The following two topics must also be promoted and followed to achieve effective purchasing.

Developing Purchasing Objectives and Controlling Purchasing Practices Effectively

Purchasing management must set up objectives to increase efficiency and effectiveness by using measures such as employing qualified staff, planning adequate budgeting, applying advanced technologies, providing professional staff training, and improving the decision-making process. The capabilities of company's purchasing efforts are crucial to achieve increased competitiveness on quality, pricing, and operation.

For example, to prevent affecting product quality and customer satisfaction because of cost reduction, companies need to take actions from either upstream suppliers and manufacturers or downstream end-users to find out any operational improvements by removing redundant expenses out of their supply chain practices. Once costs can be effectively reduced by using proper purchasing functions in the supply chain, companies can compete by benefiting from their newly acquired strategic advantage.

Managing the Purchasing Cycle and Its Process Efficiently

During purchasing operations, purchasing can be executed as a cycle of repeated activities from identifying required products, their sourcing, data collection, supplier selection, to performance reviews. These processes are complicated and vary depending on whether purchasing is considering acquiring new items or repeat ones based on a value analysis of "**Make or Buy**."**

New product development will require time, labor, cost, and may even increase risk, but could result in more revenues and profits on higher sales if the new items meet customer needs. As for repeat items, factors regarding purchasing are relatively reliable from approved sources and suppliers, but the effects of outdated products might affect customer satisfaction potentially resulting in lower sales and profits. Therefore, the purchasing process cycle is an important factor for minimizing operation costs and avoiding decision errors.

Most companies waste too much time and energy on irrelevant events. According to the *Pareto Principle*,†† many companies do not know why they always spend 80 percent of their time managing only 20 percent of their purchasing activities. Most of the weakness in purchasing cycles can be removed by adopting online requisitioning systems, online procurement cards, online electronic purchasing applications, online ordering systems, and electronic data interchange tools.[8]

In current supply chain settings, companies have confirmed that they can create values and core advantages against competition through unique and efficient purchasing processes.

** **A make-or-buy decision** is the act of choosing between manufacturing a product in-house or purchasing it from an external supplier. In a make-or-buy decision, the most important factors to consider are part of quantitative analysis, such as the associated costs of production and whether the business has the capacity to produce at required levels. Ref: Make-Or-Buy Decision http://investopedia.com/terms/m/make-or-buy-decision.asp#ixzz4uBtHJEW2

†† The **Pareto principle** is a common principle in business management; for example, "80 percent of your sales come from 20 percent clients. Many business executives have cited the 80/20 rule as a tool to maximize business efficiency.

Notes

1. Narayanan and Raman (2004, p. 172).
2. Chopra and Peter (2001, pp. 193–95).
3. Spear and Bowen (1999, p. 118).
4. Liker and David (2005, p. 8).
5. Miyashita and David (1994, pp. 134–45).
6. Krajewski and Ritzman (2002, p. 502).
7. Monczka, Robert, and Robert (2002, pp. 51–55).
8. Ibid, pp. 51–55.

References

Chopra, S., and M. Peter. 2001. *SCM: Strategy, Planning, and Operation, Part 3, Chapter 8: Managing Uncertainty in a Supply Chain, 8.3: Impact of Supply Uncertainty on Safety Inventory*, 193–95. London, UK: Pearson Education.

Krajewski, L.J., and L.P. Ritzman. 2002. *Operations Management: Strategy and Analysis, Part 5, Chapter 11: SCM,* 502. London, UK: Pearson Education.

Liker, J., and M. David. 2005. *The Toyota Way Field Book: Chapter 1, Background to the Field Book*, 8. New York, NY: Mcgraw-hill.

Miyashita, K., and R. David. 1994. *Keiretsu: Inside the Hidden Japanese Conglomerates*, 134–45. New York, NY: Mcgraw-hill.

Monczka, R., T. Robert, and H. Robert. *2002. Purchasing and SCM: Section 1, Understanding the Procurement and Sourcing Process, Chapter 2: The Purchasing Process*, 2nd ed., 23, 51–55. Boston, MA: Cengage Learning.

Narayanan, V.G., and A. Raman. 2004. "Align Incentives in the Supply Chains." *Harvard Business Review on SCM*, p. 172. Brighton, Massachusetts: Harvard Business Review.

SCMITT BERTEL. January 30, 2017. "It's Official: Volkswagen Is World's Largest Automaker In 2016. Or Maybe Toyota." *Forbes Magazine.* https://forbes.com/sites/bertelschmitt/2017/01/30/its-official-volkswagen-worlds-largest-automaker-2016-or-maybe-toyota/#562fddc176b0

Spear, S.J., and H.K. Bowen. 1999. "Decoding the DNA of the Toyota Production System." *Harvard Business Review on SCM*, 118. Brighton, Massachusetts: Harvard Business Review.

CHAPTER 11

New Supply Chain Strategy Approaches

Introduction

Since the early 1980s, when the Japanese introduced their just-in-time system for industrial operations, business settings changed in many ways to manage better the supply chain. Difficulties regarding process simplification, inventory control, quality assurance, on-time delivery, and fast service resulted from this new approach-driven business environment. To effectively figure out the problems that companies where facing, they needed to find new ideas for efficient application of their supply chain strategies to address those unique challenges.[1]

The Chinese Example

In China, those problems were phenomenal. Situations in the Asia-Pacific region have significantly changed after China reopened its gate to private sectors via its economic reform. Trends in domestic developments and international trade in China created important demand on sourcing raw materials, raising funds, developing technology, improving transportation, and seeking skilled labor.

In the 1980s, the Chinese market went through a dramatic shift in industrial productivity and operational capability. Both inbound volumes of products moving domestically across provinces and outbound products shipping internationally increased its trade surplus and national wealth. However, this growth seriously challenged supply chain practices across all Chinese industries. High demand on the supply chain to transport and deliver goods in a timely manner were forcing the introduction of new business models and the use of larger ship sizes and faster transportation services, resulting in increased shipment capacity and reduced repetitive loading costs. Furthermore, more substantial material delivery by air or surface still encountered problems such as traffic congestion at ports or highways, tighter spaces at terminal warehouses, limited capability on truckloads, or even the need of building new facilities.

SCM Performance Threats

The earlier factors threaten Chinese supply chain performance because of the resulting longer shipment loading times, longer lead times in ordering material, and longer wait times in delivering finished goods. Because of those problems, costs, time to process, and operation deficiency were expected to increase, and likely, to directly affect supply chain activities. Therefore, some strategies have been developed and adopted to improve the physical merchandise flow, decrease operation costs, and hasten shipment delivery in supply chain operations.

One of the most common strategies was to diversify port usage by using alternative ports. For example, Kaohsiung is the largest and busiest port in Taiwan. In 2015, this port ranked on the 13th place of the world's top 20 ports in handling cargo containers* causing important congestions on the discharge and reload of goods.[2]

It is interesting to note that the largest container ports in the United States (those of Los Angeles and Long Beach) were ranked 19th, and 20th on this list, with a volume almost four times lower than China's most prominent container ports. [Ibid]

If the transportation model can be redesigned to fit in the supply chain by switching cargo to dispersed locations like that of the second largest Taiwan's port, the Taichung Port in central Taiwan, problems related to extra costs and time-consuming shipment operations could be solved rapidly. Additionally, shipment diversification can also lower risk related to labor strikes, port delays, terrorist attacks, customs clearance,

---

* List of the world's busiest container ports (ports with container terminals that specialize in handling goods transported in shipping containers) by total number of actual twenty-foot equivalent units (TEUs) transported through the port. https://en.wikipedia.org/wiki/List_of_busiest_container_ports

and terminal deficiency. Although dispersing goods through various neighboring ports may result in some economies of scale by requiring additional coordination, exchanging extra data, and increasing administrative expenses, effective supply chain practices can help make up for these weaknesses.

Addressing issues associated with a proper distribution function is another strategy to improve supply chain performance. Companies need to reconsider the location, number, size, functionality, and diversification of their distribution networks to expect receiving more quickly products under their control. This involves adding facilities near alternative ports to match the supply chain redesign. As a result, distribution networks will not only need to assess market share and transportation requirements, but also consider fast delivery and cost expenditures.

In China, companies have learned to build facilities such as distribution centers or transfer stations along coasts to meet market demand. Most goods under current distribution network redesign can be guaranteed to be delivered within one week from the distribution center to other provinces through their supply chain.

By applying advanced technology on demand forecasting and planning execution, the flow of physical distribution and information exchange can be expedited to support business development and to better manage supply chain operations. Technological systems, such as I2 Technologies and CAPS Logistics[†] have helped develop numerous new business opportunities and increased market share in dispersed areas across national borders.[3]

Globalizing product distribution involves more transportation costs, better service, and higher inventory levels throughout the supply chain; however, benefits by using proper management solutions can help enhance the mobility of supply chain operations. Strategies to get the right goods to the right customer at the right time and the right price are the best weapons to competing successfully. Companies in the supply chain are also more likely to maintain their competitiveness in costs reduction, quality assurance, comprehensive service, fast delivery, and technical support by using unique SCM strategies.

[†] **CAP Logistics** is a mission-critical transportation logistics tracking provider serving heavy industries worldwide. http://caplogistics.com/aboutus/

When designing supply chain networks, the matter of a trade-off between cost and customer service is always hard to balance. Supply chain operations must set goals to minimize costs while providing satisfactory services to the customers. No doubt, SCM is still facing challenges and pressures. Many new strategies must be redesigned to reduce the cost to run a business, fasten goods delivery, better manage inventory levels, and improve customer service.

SCM Price Analysis

"Time is money."

Every company's objective is making a profit for its stakeholders. Members in the supply chain contribute their time to their chain network and make chain operations successfully by means of a team-based work. They get what they work for.

Figuring out the cost of any operation is not easy. Cost always affects product value, quality, technology, performance, and service. One of the main company responsibilities is to ensure that the cost of goods is reasonable and affordable. Commodity costs can seriously influence their price-setting, which can lead to customer acceptance or rejection when launching that product. Accurate evaluation linking the cost of the product and the price a company expects for it is a challenge in all industries.

In the supply chain, companies must first rightly apply the concept of cost and price analysis. If a company increases its product production volume, resources such as raw materials, utility, and parts will increase accordingly. Increased product volume also causes higher production costs. Variable cost behavior is directly correlated to production volume, whereas the more products the company produces, the lower the cost per product unit. Figure 11.1 illustrates the relation of production costs to production volume.[4]

The equation for cost calculation shown previously is as follows:

$$T_C = T_{FC} + (U_{VC} * X)$$

Where
T_C = Total cost;

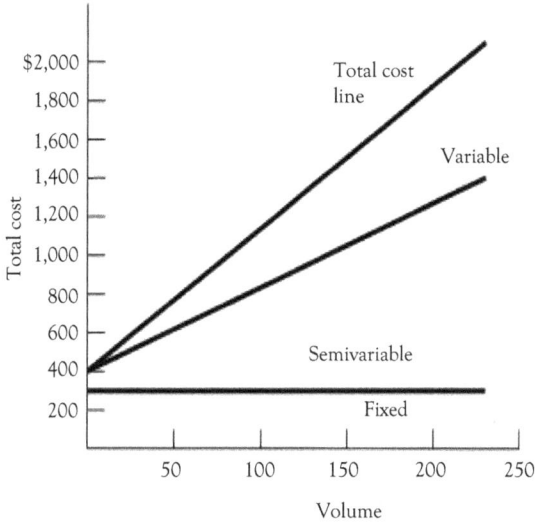

Figure 11.1 Relation of production costs to production volume

T_{FC} = Total fixed cost;
U_{VC} = Unit variable cost; and
X = Number of unit.

The average cost per product unit is the total cost divided by total volume. In contrast, price analysis consists of analyzing the cost of production as it relates to the cost of the entire supply chain operation. After adding the profit, the analysis can suggest a price for a product at a reasonable and profitable level across the supply chain.

In addition to the costs listed previously, factors from external environments will also affect the targeted market price. Product price often fluctuates according to competition and the balance of demand and supply. When demand exceeds supply, the market will switch to the supplier side, and the price will go up depending on the volume supplied. Conversely, in a buyer market, the price will usually decrease. However, different factors based on various market structures and economic conditions can affect product price. Product price is solely guided by the forces of demand and supply, according to the laws of demand and supply.[5]

Figure 11.2 presents a specific model of supply and demand, which can readily determine the product price by using corresponding algebraic calculation.

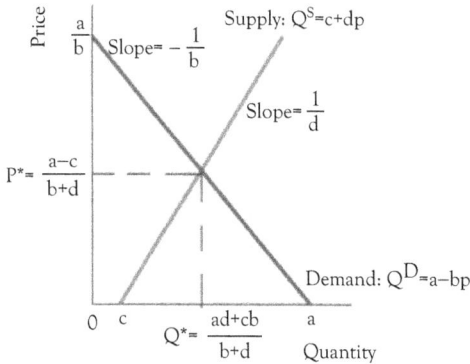

Figure 11.2 Relation of total costs to volume

Consider the following demand and supply curves:

Demand: Q^D = a − bp;

Supply: Q^S = c + dp.

Where Q^D is quantity demanded, Q^S is quantity supplied, a, b, c, and d are positive constants, and p is the price.

According to the ascending and descending lines on the graph, the product price can be quickly determined by computing the intersection point of these two lines. Eventually, market forces will affect the end-price based on a balance between demand and supply.

A balanced price means that the price paid by the customer will equal to the price received by the supplier.

The equation can be rewritten as:

a−bp = c + dp

Which leads to the solution for p as

p = (a−c)/(b+d).

As a result, the price (p) of the product is the money that must be paid to get one unit of that product.

After analyzing the cost and price product factors, it is increasingly important to consider the implications of cost and price management from the supply chain perspective. Because the traditional way of focusing cost from a company's point of view is not enough, the company must act on reducing costs both upstream and downstream of its supply chain.

Any cost-reduction effort across the whole supply chain will benefit the whole chain. The more costs the companies can save from the collaboration among supply chain operations, the more profits they can gain.

Breakeven Analysis

Finally, a breakeven analysis is applied to determine the optimal price.

The equation for the breakeven chart in Figure 11.3 can be presented as[6]:

$$T_R = T_C$$
$$T_R = P * X$$
$$T_C = T_{FC} + (U_{VC} * X)$$

Where

T_R = Total revenue

T_C = Total costs of production

P = Unit price

X = Number of units

T_{FC} = Total fixed cost

U_{VC} = Unit variable cost

The equation for the breakeven volume (X) can be reached as:

$$X = T_{FC} \div (P - U_{VC})$$

After the breakeven volume is found, the minimum volume required to make the expected profit is easy to calculate.

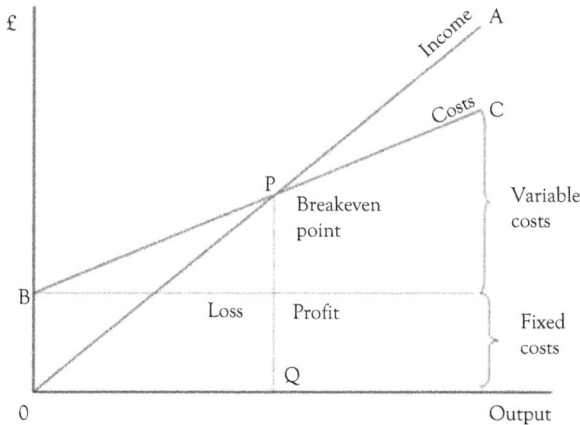

Figure 11.3 Breakeven chart

$$P = \text{Profit/loss} + (U_{VC} * X) + T_{FC}\} \div X$$

Breakeven analysis can help companies identify ideal product quantity and verify profit margins by improving supply chain performance and its operational efficiency.

At the breakeven point P, the revenues resulting from the sales are equal to the expenses spent on the product. The point is mainly based on total costs, which consist of variable costs that change when the volume changes and fixed costs that do not relate directly to the production volume. Beyond this point, a company can realize whether it generates a profit or a loss.

Notes

1. Ayers (2000).
2. Wang (2007).
3. Fontanella (2000).
4. Anthony, Hawkins, and Merchant (1999, p. 490).
5. Gagan and Lipsey (2005, pp. 68–69).
6. Anthony, Hawkins, and Merchant (1999, pp. 499–506).

References

Anthony, R.N., D.F. Hawkins, and K.A. Merchant. 1999. *Accounting: Text and Cases, Part 2, Chapter 16: The Behavior of Costs*, 10th ed., 490. New York, NY: Mcgraw-hill.

Anthony, R.N., D.F. Hawkins, and K.A. Merchant. 1999. *Accounting: Text and Cases, Part 2, Chapter 16: The Behavior of Costs*, 10th ed., 499–506. New York, NY: Mcgraw Hill.

Ayers, J.B. 2000. "A Primer on Supply Chain Management." *Information Strategy: The Executive's Journal*, http://ayers-consulting.com/Download/01-Primer-2nd-version-2000.pdf

Fontanella, S.J. 2000. "Supply Chain Planning and Execution: CAPS Logistics to Power ship Logix LX." http://utilitiesindustry.com/Content/View.asp?pmillid=6739

Gagan, C.T.S., and R.G. Lipsey. 2005. *Microeconomics, Part 2, Chapter 3: Demand Supply, and Price*, 11th ed., 68–69. London, UK: Pearson Education.

Wang, K.-E. 2007. "Upgrade the Tranship Competitiveness for Kaohsiung Port." http://mtedi.org.tw/%C2%B2%B0T%B8%EA%AE%C6/%B2%C4%A4 G%A4Q%A4T%B4%C1/23-3.htm

CHAPTER 12

Creating an Effective SCM

Introduction

We have seen so far that SCMs can yield substantial benefits for companies in handling issues such as sourcing materials, product distribution, marketing channel, information sharing, and customer demand. Furthermore, SCM practices help companies improve internal efficiencies and increase profit. Finally, SCM also prevents companies from wasting valuable time, labor, and resources. Effective system re-engineering can trigger supply chain operations going forward. Operational efficiency can be highly enhanced by adopting a range of unique management solutions including resources integration, technical support, inventory control, quality assurance, systemic coordination, and customer service.

Because of globalization and technological prevalence, activities and events are linked together through point-to-point and react to market demand and customer needs worldwide. The current trend in the application of SCM is in forcing companies to change their ways from running their business traditionally to be able to respond quickly to market demand. Therefore, it is extremely important to effectively integrate one's operations with external systems of suppliers, manufacturers, intermediaries, and customers. On the other hand, SCMs also promise to expedite the productivity and profitability by applying useful expertise, knowledge, intelligence, and data exchange into chain activities for business developments.

According to the Advanced Market Research (**AMR**),* companies that are best at managing their supply chain are outperforming other

_____
* AMR http://amr-research.com/

S&P 500 companies.[†] AMR found that the top 25 companies embracing demand-driven supply networks, which are "agile enough to respond to customer demand," are like good athletes and "usually win." AMR states that companies building toward the supply chain model are measurably better on an operational excellence and of innovation excellence.[1]

The key point here is not how companies understand SCM's importance, but how they can create an effective SCM to face their competition.

Keys to a Successful SCM

A successful supply chain is a comprehensive and interdependent entity, which can facilitate the flow of physical materials, information, and capital back and forth from supplier to end-user by making it more efficient. SCM enables a better management of the supply chain by optimizing business operations and maximizing business profits. To reach the business goals and to reinforce competitiveness, the supply chain performance must be enhanced by considering a couple of key issues in the current business settings.

The creation of an effective SCM depends on the effectiveness of successfully addressing three of its dimensions: structure dimension, infrastructure dimension, and performance dimension.

The Structure Dimension

The structure dimension of a supply chain includes configuration, connection, inventory, and logistics to efficiently cover the supply chain operations.[2] Configuration refers to the physical arrangements of the proper process, consisting of many factors such as policy setting, system design, cost structure, human resources, and facility selection.

When companies in the supply chain decide to set up a business model for their specific configuration, they have to figure out the next

---

[†] The **Standard & Poor's 500**, often abbreviated as the **S&P 500**, or just "the S&P," is an American stock market index based on the market capitalizations of 500 large companies having common stock listed on the NYSE or NASDAQ. https://en.wikipedia.org/wiki/S%26P_500_Index

step of how to connect each different member at a dispersed location. How to efficiently match and link different processes among chain activities is a big challenge. Once products can be delivered fast to meet market demand, inventory plays a critical role as a buffer for sufficient on-time replenishment. To maintain the inventory balance is hard within supply chain activities.

For example, retailers may keep more inventories on hand for peak demands like during the Christmas period. They will put orders with lead-times to drive manufacturers to hold higher inventories of raw materials earlier than usual, which can be often risky because forecasting market demand is not always an easy task. If signals from retailers are incorrect, manufacturers may encounter losses because of higher inventories, which may dangerously disrupt the manufacturers' site operations. In turn, the effectiveness of supply chain may also be hurt by unexpected interruptions.

Another factor to consider is distribution and transportation in the supply chain operations logistics. Cost and delivery time can be reduced based on the system design via efficient distribution and choice of transportation options by air or by surface. Proper logistics practices also have a close relationship with inventory issue; they are affecting each other proportionally.

The Infrastructure Dimension

Collaboration and coordination are critical factors to ensure that chain members function well with each other. Cooperative supply chain operations can share knowledge and information, quickly develop new products, capture business opportunities, and respond to customer demands. Suppliers, manufacturers, distributors, retailer, and customers can simultaneously exchange collected data, share analytical information, and act timely on product movements. If not, businesses in any industry might encounter tremendous pressures resulting from their markets.

Business tendencies will motivate all chain members to work together in a seamless manner to better face unavoidable competition challenges. An adequate approach to collaboration and coordination allows chain members to perceive a sort of efficiency throughout their supply chain.

Their core competencies can be achieved by understanding customer needs and satisfying market demand after collaborative operations are applied.

Introduction of SCM application systems, software, processes, and frameworks may encourage separate chain members working together to develop all supply operations cooperatively, from sourcing, manufacturing, planning, distributing, and delivering, to servicing. If chain members' common goals can be reached by effective cooperation, they will be willing to support different operations and work on compatible environments in their supply chain rather than just focus on their individual needs.

The Performance Dimension

Many companies use Internet and Intranet networking systems to communicate their inventory levels, delivery speed, and customer needs for secured inventory replenishments. As a result, they often maintain significant inventories to meet market demand and to keep balanced inventory levels among chain members, particularly in peak seasons. Measurements of customer requirements can not only satisfy safe inventory levels but also reduce transportation charges markedly and increase inventory efficiency.

In addition to customer requirement measurements, other measurements such as information exchange, process simplification, resources sharing, financial achievement, and system integration, are also practical tools that can be used to evaluate and verify the effectiveness of SCMs. Companies must understand how market competition affects their business competitiveness and what chain operation influence their customers' satisfaction.

Notes

1. Business Periodicals, Manufacturing and Technology News: Best at SCM also Lead in Stock Market (2006).
2. Kim (2005, pp. 2–10).

References

Business Periodicals, Manufacturing and Technology News: Best at SCM also Lead in Stock Market. March 3, 2006. http://allbusiness.com/finance/871403-1. html

Kim, B. 2005. *Mastering Business in Asia, SCM: Chapter 1, SCM: Creating Value for the Customers*, 2–10. Hoboken, New Jersey: John Wiley & Sons.

CHAPTER 13

Managing the Supply Chain

Introduction

Companies in the supply chain must commit to operational excellence and superior performance under high competition. Nobody can afford to waste resources on improper operations or spend extra time on tedious processes. Lack of supply chain planning and integration will not only result in poor performance and lower profitability but also in loss of market share and loyal customers. Therefore, after understanding the importance and keys to creating effective SCMs, how to manage better supply chain is another critical factor.

In practice, operations and processes in a supply chain network are interdependent. Supply chain members continuously need to share information, exchange experience, and coordinate procedures across various activities as an integrated entity. Well-organized integration in a supply chain is not an easy endeavor. Employees at either end of the chain have separate perspectives, many skills, and diverse expertise; they experience pressure at many levels, face distinctive difficulties and challenges, and use separate data and resources. Picking up any of those factors will no doubt affect the smooth operation of supply chain activities. In addition to human factors, other factors such as the differences in systems, software, data, process, and industry practices, also influence supply chain performance.

A beginning step in managing a supply chain is the development of standard processes, procedures, systems, information, and goals within chain members. Integrated software such as **Oracle's PeopleSoft** applications* with common planning and initiatives can be applied to connect

---

* **Oracle's PeopleSoft applications** are designed to address the most complex business requirements. They provide comprehensive business and industry solutions, enabling organizations to increase productivity, accelerate business performance, and provide a lower cost of ownership. http://oracle.com/us/products/applications/peoplesoft-enterprise/overview/index.html

the dispersed activities in different parts of the entire supply chain. **PeopleSoft** is designed to professionally integrate market, distribution, resource, finance, business information, operations, e-business data, and customer service into a streamlined, innovative manner. The Oracle PeopleSoft application is a suitable solution for growing businesses working cooperatively within their supply chain. Different events marked by arrowed lines throughout a supply chain are integrated at a central facility and spread out efficiently with shared processes, materials, and data.[1] Formerly isolated functions in the supply chain can now work as a whole. Each member can cooperate with other members, working as a cross-functional team, which will eventually develop joint strategies to achieve business goals and synchronize market approaches.

The development of integrated practices has to cover every member and location by using standard criteria and requirements to ensure that the goals of chain entities will never override those of the supply chain. The result is a win–win situation, the ultimate objective of better managing the supply chain. However, to create a successful integration in all respects is always hard and appears to be a big challenge.

Enterprise resources planning (**ERP**) is another application for capturing product, sales, finance, and inventory information the supply chain application needs to predict demand effectively and to optimize the flow of material throughout the chain. Indeed, those two systems serve each other well. Unfortunately, that symbiotic relationship does not translate into a smooth integration between them. In all likelihood, new supply chain implementations will not interface cleanly with current ERP systems. A company has to rework its ERP system to match the supply chain system for those two systems to work together.[2] Therefore, a comprehensive integration of SCM systems and processes is very critical for better management of a supply chain.

Another approach for better management of a supply chain is to understand the role of every chain entity and to create a win–win situation for all involved. In many industries, the dysfunction of supply chain operations often results from confusion over the role each chain member plays. For example, retailers are always expecting to sell more items at peak periods and ask for adequate supplies within reasonable pricing ranges inside lead-times that will meet their needs. Because of the bullwhip effect, suppliers, manufacturers, or wholesalers may suffer potential risks of demand variability. They may maintain productivity and inventory at secured levels to avoid uncertainties. This behavior may result in confusing their role in the chain, which might influence the benefits of the entire supply chain operation. Since chain members are focusing on their individual benefits rather than that of all chain members, they may consequently suffer a loss rather than a profit. Therefore, some of the best advice to avoid this behavior is to develop win–win situations for all chain members.

Win–win situations are mostly reached through a contractual framework. Contracts or agreements based on a legal arrangement or long-term partnership should be fostered to allow mutual trust and respect for best chain collaboration and coordination. Companies in the supply chain will then get what they need based on market demand and customer requirements.

Another factor to better managing supply chain is setting up clear and detailed criteria and specifications for supply chain activities. Most companies often think that what they do in business is based on the way they used to perform independently. They might forget that practices such as market trends, contract protocols, management solutions, and technological tools may be increasingly changing. Companies are required to not only comply with the criteria and specifications imposed by the supply chain agreements they entered into, to best fit in the supply chain operations, but also need to accomplish tasks by adopting SCM standards to meet other chain members capabilities at same levels. Apparently, such an approach is not easy to establish overnight because of resource inadequacy, system discrepancies, software incompatibility, and process disarrangement.

Many companies have been advised to work hard on establishing more extensive, open, free, and practical communications and negotiations with their partners in the supply chain. These constructive interactions among members can be used to cultivate their business environment and to develop a healthy ambience in creating consensus on common criteria and specifications.

For example, a secured Web portal designed for chain members can be easily used to retrieve specific data at any point, 24/7. Individual chain members can quickly get the information they need from their supply chain. By adoption of the same criteria, change can immediately be posted on the portal to allow other supply chain members understand the level of change affecting them and avoid inefficient operations.

Establishing a set of criteria and specifications may involve additional time and cost. Companies may not perceive short-term results from that. However, once done, companies will gain important benefits by enhancing their core advantage and improving their enterprise profitability.

Third-Party Logistics and SCM

Companies in the supply chain cannot guarantee that everything will be done well by them. Some of the functions, such as logistics, must be rearranged using outsourcing and inventory management. They must leave warehousing, distribution, packing, and delivery to companies specializing in these areas to increase efficiency and reduce cost. No matter what their goals are, whether to remain competitive or to increase business profitability, one of the most effective solutions is seeking ways to reduce logistics costs. In general, the logistics costs can be lowered by outsourcing and inventory management.

From the perspective of resource integration, outsourcing[†] is an approach trying to transfer regular operations for superior service at lower costs. For example, Purolator has increased its business with U.S. companies selling products in Canada because Canadian customers like to have a package delivery company that can do more than delivery by including warehousing and customs brokerage. Purolator decided to consolidate its shipments destined to Canada, transport them to its border, clear them through customs, and distribute them in Canada. To address customer needs, Purolator had to cooperate with Burnham Logistics[‡] for

---

[†] **Outsourcing** is a practice used by different companies to reduce costs by transferring portions of work to outside suppliers rather than completing it internally. **Outsourcing** is an effective cost-saving strategy when used properly.

[‡] UPS Logistics and Burnham Reach Purchase Agreement. https://logisticsonline.com/doc/ups-logistics-and-burnham-reach-purchase-agre-0001

some vertical acquisitions and partnerships.[3] As a result of outsourcing, Purolator could not only concentrate time and efforts to its core business, but also reap the benefits from its partner such as well-developed logistics information systems, experienced logistics personnel, customs facilities, cross-borders warehousing, extensive distributions, and lower transportation charges.

Another critical approach used to decrease logistics costs is inventory control by working with third-party inventory control logistics partners such as **3PLs**.[§] Companies expecting to minimize stock levels in their supply chain need to pay more attention to inventory control, which can result in satisfying market demand through effective forecasting techniques.

Companies in a supply chain can use those integration solutions between them and their logistics providers to achieve important benefits. After cooperating with logistics partners as a group in the supply chain, companies tend to achieve bilateral profitability resulting from the efforts of reducing delivery time, lowering operation costs, enhancing customer satisfactions, and improving production flexibility. In practice, to reduce logistics costs in the supply chain effectively, many companies have started to adopt highly advanced logistics solutions such as Terra Technology,[¶] IBM's ILOG,[**] Logility,[††] SAP's SmartOps,[‡‡] and ToolsGroup,[§§] to name a few of the most common ones.

Terra Technology's demand-sensing solution, for example, is an expert system, which can augment and improve traditional demand planning programs by combining real-time data with advanced mathematics to cut forecast errors. Terra relies on a pattern-recognition model to help companies improve the accuracy of sales forecasts. For most food companies,

---

[§] A **3PL** (third-party logistics) is a provider of outsourced logistics services. Logistic services encompass anything that involves management of the way resources are moved to the areas where they are required. The term comes from the military.

[¶] http://supplychain247.com/company/terra_technology

[**] https://www-01.ibm.com/software/info/ilog/

[††] https://logility.com/

[‡‡] https://SAP.com

[§§] https://toolsgroup.com/

safety stock is 35 to 40 percent of their inventory, which is their upper limit against forecast errors. If forecast errors can be reduced by half, it would mean 20 percent less safety stock will need to be maintained.

Procter & Gamble (P&G)†† is also using this type of model in Europe and spread it to all its worldwide locations. By improving forecast accuracy one to six weeks out, P&G expected to reduce inventory levels by 10 percent.[4]

According to AT Kearney:

[In 2106], overall spending on logistics dropped despite a rise in energy prices. This marked the second straight year in which the two have moved in opposite directions, indicating energy prices are no longer the primary factor in logistics costs. AT Kearney suggested that consumers have become the driving force behind logistics spending, and 2016's results confirm the powerful effect of rising consumer demand for e-commerce deliveries. While overall transportation costs fell 0.7 percent last year, spending on package delivery services jumped 10 percent. Parcel and express delivery has surpassed railroads as the second-largest logistics sector behind motor freight. Meanwhile, energy-sensitive pipelines and railroads saw rates and volumes stall or drop as oil prices remained at historically low levels despite the upturn in 2016. Storage expenditures rose 1.8 percent and as important as the financial carrying cost of inventory.[5]

Therefore, companies wanting to improve their bottom line need to focus on inventory management and forecasting implementation. Controlling excessive inventory by using advanced forecasting skills can avoid inventory responsibility from shifting backward in the supply chain and ensure buffer inventories among supply chain members remain well-managed. If inventory issues cannot be managed well, the resulting negative effect on total costs, supply visibility, timely delivery, and service levels will become severe threats to profitability.

––––––––––

†† https://us.pg.com/

Lowering inventory and improving outsourcing have continued to be key goals for companies to cooperate with third-party logistics partners. Marketplace demand shift can be so variable that even the best companies might suffer excessive inventory costs or lose profits because of enduring unintentionally out-of-stock products. Figuring out inventory problems by optimizing solutions in association with third-party logistics partners is critical and feasible. If companies could collect adequate data from their supply chain members to precisely forecast market demand by using proper techniques, inventory optimization for upstream chain members will be achieved straightforwardly and maintained at a safety level.

Improved capability using third-party logistics allows companies to react quickly to changing market requirements. As a result, not only the logistics costs inside the supply chain will be reduced in light of the efforts of outsourcing and inventory control, but companies can also achieve improved resource integration, efficiency enhancement, fill rate fulfillment, and on-time delivery. Companies have been aware that these business improvements trends can ultimately benefit their supply chain. From a third-party logistics perspective, those practices have resulted in better customer service, better transportation arrangement, better process flexibility, and better resource integration. All those results also contribute to lower total costs. For third-party logistics providers and companies in the supply chain, the outcome is a win–win situation.

Implementation of Demand Planning and Sales Forecasting in SCMs

Since global business is growing fast and is complicated, supply chain activities have been fully involved with sophisticated operations in cutting increasing costs of inventory, logistics, or human resources. However, a movement to best reduce costs is no longer enough for supply chain members. The most prominent issue before them is how they can better manage their supply chain of the goods they will be sourcing, manufacturing, storing, and distributing in advance. This problem merely results in a need of better demand planning and sales forecasting. Every manufacturer along a complex supply chain likes to produce goods exactly to meet market demand; every retailer also attempts to prepare its inventory to meet customer needs. The challenge is how the market can be forecasted and planned efficiently.

In many situations products are produced and delivered slower than spiking demands because forecasting problems are very complicated to implement effectively, especially during demands spike. As a result, this challenge might cause important supply chain disruptions or even dysfunctions. By recognizing that issues of demand and forecast will both affect cost and profit, companies begin to pay more attention to demand planning and market trends analysis. The outcome may result in new policy provisions for the supply chain.

Adequate demand planning and sales forecasting may also result in other benefits such as corresponding warehousing, inventory, and transportation cost reductions. Manufacturers cooperating in the supply chain can also benefit by adequately managing large uncertain orders in planning much earlier, a practice that allows them to predict orders and to integrate production resources in advance. As a result, the additional costs of quick sourcing, expanding production lines, overtime work, and expedited shipment can be reduced to fill up the orders and to increase productivity. These premanaging processes derived from proper approaches to demand planning and sales forecast can decrease manufacturers' costs and increase their market share. Multinational transactions require substantially tighter collaboration and coordination among complex trading partner networks. In response, companies are building business processes, organizations, and technology portfolios that allow them to manage this complexity and the ever-present uncertainty of supply and demand.[6]

Supply chain management is not just about forecasting; it covers the entire demand management in any supply chain, which consists of mainly issues of demand planning and sales forecast. For examples, business retailers in a supply chain can be directly affected by uncertain demand because they have to deal with their end-users face-to-face, which can cause variable and unpredictable demand forecasting. Nevertheless, manufacturers in the supply chain can modify their operations by improving their demand planning and sales forecast capabilities. Because of developing various techniques, systems, and processes, these practices can profoundly affect cost reduction and order fulfillment.

However, if for example, the forecast results with a +/– 10 percent error, the retailer might place an order with its supplier (the wholesaler) for 11,000 units (<<10,000 × 0.1>> + 10,000), even though it has better demand management forecasting skills. These extra 1,000 units of safety stock must be ordered to meet the expected forecasting error. The ensuing numbers in the supply chain could increase further. Based on 11,000 units, the wholesaler (the importer) in turn will also increase the forecasted demand to 12,100 units (<<11,000 × 0.1>> + 11,000) by applying an identical forecasting error of approximately +/– 10 percent. When the order is placed, the number of units will reach 13,310 units (<<12,100 × 0.1>> + 12,100). Therefore, the order to the manufacturer will be inflated again to 14,641 units (<<13,310 × 0.1>> + 13,310).

Even in a supply chain where forecasting error is only +/– 10 percent, the failure to forecast the market demand will add up excessive quantity in inventory carried in the supply chain to a dangerous level: a typical consequence of the bullwhip effect. Every member from retailers and importers to manufacturers in this entire supply chain only needs 10,000 units to meet the predicted demand plus 1,000 units to cover potential forecasting errors. However, the entire supply chain is carrying 11,051 units more than regular inventory requirements because of the compounded demand forecasting error resulting in 110.51 percent of the actual end-user demand. Through this example, the practice of efficient inventory forecast allows a company to realize that the implementation of demand planning and sales forecast can decrease costs and increase profit margins.

For any industry, safety stock is always there to cover for demand uncertainty. With a safety stock standard in the consumer goods industry of about 40 percent, large suppliers such as Kraft Foods may have $2 billion of stock on hand; Procter & Gamble may have double that amount.[7] If that 40 percent of stock can be reduced to 30 percent by using an effective management solution such as Terra Technology's demand sensing solution, Kraft may save $0.2 billion on the same secured inventory by improving its demand and forecast accuracy. P&G can profit much more from this same type of improvement. Therefore, more reliability on demand management along the supply chain can result in better inventory control among chain members, and less cost-carrying in the supply chain executions.

Notes

1. Fox, Mahmud, and Chris (1995).
2. Pender (2001).
3. Allen (2000).
4. Higgins (2007).
5. Vanhencxthoven et al. (2017).
6. Greg, Hillman, and Hochman (2007).
7. Paul Page (2005).

References

Allen, J. 2000. "Fast and Curious: Now that they have Mastered Express Delivery through Extensive Infrastructure, Couriers are Intrigued about the Possibilities of Handling Your Total Supply Chain." *Canadian Transportation Logistics* 103, no. 4, http://proquest.umi.com/pqdweb?did=384969941&index=3&TS=1191632440&SrchMode=1&sid=1&Fmt=3&VInst=PROD&VType=PQD&clientId=72426&RQT=309&VName=PQD&lang=en

Fox, M.S., B. Mihai, G. Mahmud, and B. Chris. 1995. *The Integrated SCM Project, Enterprise Integration Laboratory Department of Industrial Engineering.* University of Toronto, http://eil.utoronto.ca/iscm-descr.html

Greg, A., M. Hillman, and S. Hochman. 2007. "Infrastructure is Integral to Supply Chain Success: A Company's Highest Supply Chain Priorities are Demand Forecasting, Supply Planning, Inventory Management, and Sales and Operations Planning." *Industry Week*, http://findarticles.com/p/articles/mi_hb3044/is_200701/ai_n18956207

Higgins, K.T. 2007. *Supply Chain Savvy, Food Engineering.* http://foodengineeringmag.com/CDA/Archives/BNP_GUID_9-5-2006_A_10000000000000028860

Paul Page 2005. "Building Inventory's Crystal Ball." http://evansdist.com/includes/pdf/TrafficWorld8.29.05.PDF

Pender, L. 2001. "CIO: The 5 Keys to Successful SCM- Automating Your Supply Chain is the Most Difficult Software Project You'll Ever Do, 4." http://cio.com/article/30378/The_Keys_to_Successful_Supply_Chain_Management/1

Vanhencxthoven, M., S.T. Monahan, J. Ward, B. Sonthalia, and M. Zimmerman. 2017. "ATKearny, 2017 State of Logistics Report—Accelerating to Uncertainty." https://atkearney.com/transportation-travel/article?/a/2017-state-of-logistics-report-article

CHAPTER 14

Integrated SCM Strategies

Introduction

To ensure a successful supply chain operation requires a set of efficient supply chain strategies. Business development guidelines and effective SCM strategies can help companies build up firm foundations and improve their competitive advantage. Through SCM practices, companies can compete effectively and expect to achieve sustainability for long-term business growth. If companies try to satisfy the needs of their target markets, they must explore what strategies they should adopt to manage better their business and expand their customer base. The key issues they have to address are integrating their supply chain activities, operations, and systems into a solid mechanism based on their competitive advantage. After effective integration, the members in the supply chain can coordinate and collaborate with each other to create products and to satisfy customers throughout their network.

Business strategies can affect marketing, production, finance, and human resources. Altogether, strategies must be aligned within the associated supply chain to enhance supply chain members' competitiveness. Traditionally, features of the product itself have dominated in determining its market position. Presently products increasingly compete with the supply chains that deliver them.[1] By using unique supply chain strategies, companies can devise potential and business opportunities to achieve a competitive position.

As the market has pushed supply chains to shift from cost-oriented considerations to customer-centered efforts, this transformation means that companies need to strengthen their supply chain with systematic strategies to improve customer-focus transactions. They also need to automate their core processes to reduce errors and redundancies, and to improve their efficiency. Lastly, they need to tailor their processes and infrastructure to suit different products, customers, markets, partner, and timeframes.[2]

Thinking comprehensively about the SCM effect on business development is critical. Because of excellent supply chain strategies, the accomplishment and success throughout the supply chain will benefit not only the member companies, but also their partners and customers.

Internal Integration Between Chain Members and Their Customers

SCM has many elements associated with its customers or end-users. Companies have been influenced in their business development because of customer-oriented concerns. However, many of them are still not cognizant of the customer focus importance. Companies need to recognize how they can develop their operation settings so that they are designed not only to achieve better functionality, but also to focus on their customers' concerns better.

For example, to integrate complex procedures through well-engineering processes in a supply chain by linking downstream data such as customer demand, market requirements, and quality specifications is a very critical step. If many of supply chain information flows such as marketing plans, inventory levels, transportation management, warehousing planning, packaging designs, production models, and source selections from downstream to upstream of a supply chain (or vice versa), the supply chain could be automatically and efficiently coordinated and implemented with each partner resulting in numerous advantages to benefit the supply chain, especially on the customer side.

From the market point of view, a customer-oriented flow will help chain activities pinpointing product portfolios so that they reflect market requirements. SCM operations will be illustrated as a collaborate processes of supply chain flows from sourcing of raw materials, product customization or mass production, distribution design, packing requirement, to timely delivery that all seem to be tailored to meet customer demand.

In practice, competition has forced businesses to become more attune to a customer-driven network. Competition motivates members of a supply chain to keep an eye on their products proactively and to serve their target customers better by enabling a stronger position vis-a-vis their competitors in the marketplace.

Customer Relationship Management

Customer relationship management (**CRM**)* is an important component of SCM practices. CRM applies to many activities throughout the supply chain in connection to customer-centered events to establish long-term relationships with new customers and sustain the loyalty of old ones.

Committed customer relationship is one of the most sustainable advantages because of its inherent barriers to competition. The tendency of growing mass customization and personalized service is leading to a new era. Running a business by treating customers as its top priority is very crucial for business development and growth. However, to build an authentic supply chain network with a customer focus often requires different coordination and collaboration throughout the supply chain.

Most companies in a supply chain tend to focus their primary concerns on internal measurements such as cost, pricing policy, safety inventory, quality assurance, location convenience, and shipping time. They are taking these factors seriously into account and considering them as the most important parts in gaining customer recognition and praise. However, the reality is that only internal efforts are not enough. The addition of external measurements such as market trend, customer taste, price

---

* **Customer relationship management (CRM)** is an approach to managing a company's interaction with current and potential customers. It uses data analysis about customers' history with a company and to improve business relationships with customers, specifically focusing on customer retention and ultimately driving sales growth. One important aspect of the CRM approach is the systems of CRM that compile data from a range of different communication channels, including a company's website, telephone, e-mail, live chat, marketing materials, and more recently, social media. Through the CRM approach and the systems used to facilitate it, businesses learn more about their target audiences and how to best cater to their needs. However, adopting the CRM approach may also occasionally lead to favoritism within an audience of consumers, resulting in dissatisfaction among customers and defeating the purpose of CRM. Source: https://en.wikipedia.org/wiki/Customer_relationship_management

affordability, product diversity, and postsale feedback are also required to determine tangible outcomes that can reflect customer demand and expectation.

Based on a customer focus across the supply chain, different companies can work jointly to analyze customer demand data each member collects, and verify real market demand by adopting integrated systems. After comparing statistical data, which is accumulated by real daily sales, chain members can realize how well they contribute sharing their customer data. Good relationship among supply chain members, particularly regarding customer data, is critically needed for successful implementation of supply chain activities. Close customer relationship allows an organization to differentiate its product from competitors, sustain customer loyalty, and dramatically extend value to its customers.[3] However, to change companies from traditional considerations of cost interrelations to customer-oriented interactions in the supply chain operations is not a task that can be done overnight, because it requires high support and encouragement from its leadership and internal integrations of strategic directions and objectives. Effective internal integration between an enterprise and its customers is an essential factor for a prosperous SCM.

The practice concerning the supply chain goals with a customer focus is an inevitable tendency that has been formed under competition. Customer focus is also necessary for companies to provide value on products and services the customers need through the extensive integration of the supply chain. Unfortunately, notwithstanding advanced technologies and systems that are currently available to match supply chain programs, some difficulties still exist in the supply chain because of misunderstandings and traditional application of financial or operational functions rather than paying more attention to customer-oriented issues. Mismanagement because of an existing conventional human mindset and insight is one of the obstacles that challenge companies to fully accept and support the internal strategic integration inside the supply chain.

To best promote a customer-oriented approach to the supply chain networks, issues regarding the customer must be shared and consolidated in an integrated system such as the CRM one. A CRM system can be supported by data, which will benefit companies because of their customer focus. Many successful business stories such as those of

UPS, Honeywell Aerospace, HP, Fujitsu, Siemens, IBM, and Mitsubishi Motors, have justified and confirmed internal strategic integration based on a customer focus as often the best shortcut to market share and business competitiveness.

Investment of time, capital, and human resources in customer-oriented services may be significant and pricey, but the resulting benefits that can be reaped by each member of a supply chain.

External Integration with Partners in the Supply Chain

Because of customer-extensive service needs and higher product quality, companies in the supply chain must prepare well their capabilities such as skilled labor, qualified facility, advanced application systems, innovative design, and superior functionality. Additionally, they have to work closely with their external partners to satisfy market demand and customer expectations. As a result, only efforts of each supply chain member is not enough to meet these expectations. Cooperation with other external partners plays an essential role too.

For example, companies need to collaborate proactively with partners to maintain safe inventory levels to meet peak in high season demands. Companies also have to coordinate with partners to expedite customer orders delivery quickly to and from downstream chain members. External integration in the supply chain is a management issue that needs to be addressed to realize core advantages on products and services provided.

Criteria for better partner cooperation include capabilities and features to supply sourcing raw materials, produce higher product quality, regulate flexible local warehousing, provide timely shipment, and shorten lead times to meet business competitiveness objectives. Business success is emphasized by resolving cost, quality, goodwill, technology, speed, price, and service issues. Many companies are making business mistakes by focusing only on the efficiencies and processes of their operations rather than paying also attention to the importance of strategic integration with their external supply chain partners.

An efficient supply chain may not be as significant as a responsive supply chain. For example, customers may change their purchasing decisions for some unknown reason. A sudden purchasing behavior change can seriously affect the entire supply chain operations including sourcing of different raw materials and parts, production line and schedule, terminal warehousing space, packing design, and delivery speed.

Members involved in a supply chain changing environment will have not only to complete their tasks efficiently, but also to cooperate with their partners effectively by working together as a whole to satisfy the change in market demand. Otherwise, the loss of market share may be inevitable. Therefore, active supply chain operations must not only address issues of performance, but also emphasize the importance of strategic integration among supply chain members. Several actions and strategies can be considered to overcome those kinds of external integration problems.

The following managerial actions can help maintain supply chain profits and moderate the bullwhip effect[4]:

1. Align goals and incentives
2. Enhance information accuracy
3. Improve operational performance
4. Design pricing strategies to stabilize orders
5. Build partnerships and trust

Even though chain members agree with the actions listed previously and recognize that effective external integration is critical and valuable, efforts to achieve and maintain integration are difficult. In most practical situations, companies may expect others to cooperate with them by signing a contract. However, in practice, it is impossible to ask for any cooperation by only relying on a contract. Building up mutual trust with partners through external integration can help resolve those type of issues typically not included in a contract.

From a technical point of view, external integration with partners in the supply chain can be achieved by adopting advanced management solutions such as UPS's Flex Global View,[†] a web-based event-tracking and reporting tool that allows authorized users to check the status of supply chain activities, relying on data files transmitted continually from a variety of participants in the supply chain.[5]

[†] See: https://ups.com/cw/en/tracking/flex-global-view.page

By applying adequate functions and processes throughout the supply chain, external integration with partners can be effectively implemented in a business setting to use chain resources fully and to smoothly streamline information processing and product flow inside the supply chain. Because of the proper partner external integration, companies can enhance their competitiveness and satisfy their customers.

Information Integration Among Chain Members

SCM is dealing with the right product delivery to the right place at the right time and the right price. To ensure product delivery goals are met, exchange and sharing of information applied in the supply chain are vital operations that must be achieved efficiently. Information flow in connection to products, market, resources, techniques, and services, among chain members, can be viewed as essential indicators reflecting the coordination and efficiency of a supply chain.

Thanks to advanced technological improvements in information systems, these challenges have been shifted from how information is exchanged efficiently to what information is critical to share with chain members, and subsequently, benefit the supply chain. Developing the information systems capability can help supply chain reduce information distortion and increase operational efficiency.

For example, information regarding market demand and inventory control can be carefully managed among chain members to efficiently reduce the bullwhip effect and operational costs in the supply chain. Just in time is one of the preferred systems designed to assist with a rapid market demand information distribution and to focus on the reduction of lead times and inventory cost by using fast and accurate operation tactics.

Many other techniques have also been developed and applied to assist a workable flow of information in the supply chain providing a variety of information such as materials planning, inventory control, product diversity, sales services, price analysis, purchasing functions, supplier evaluations, and third-party logistics.

The application of collaborative planning, forecasting, and replenishment (**CPFR**) by using database management systems (**DBMS**) and electronic data interchange (**EDI**) are other examples of techniques adopted to better manage information throughout the supply chain. Shared information can vary from strategic to tactical and from logistic activities to general market and customer information.[6] As a result, information integration can help chain members from upstream suppliers to downstream end-users work collaboratively to minimize the waste of limited resources and maximize the efficiency of supply chain execution.

Information integration arises from the application of different practices that can strengthen competitiveness required in the supply chain. Rapidity and accuracy of information are crucial factors that determine how a supply chain is going to function better and fit its business setting. Furthermore, credibility is a key factor in the process of information integration because each member in the supply chain may have an incentive or intention to distort its information for its benefit. These types of transgressions may influence the receiver's decision making and policy setting resulting in reducing effective information integration in the supply chain. Because of misunderstandings, chain members who receive inadequate information are likely to stop sharing their information with their partners, which will consequently hurt overall supply chain activities. Hence, mechanisms that can diminish such opportunistic behavior while allowing for increased benefits from information sharing are critical to the creation of efficient supply chain.[7]

Establishing an adequate supervision of information integration between supply chain members is quite tricky. Information exchange and sharing across the supply chain is easily accomplished by applying technical solutions, but hard to be executed because of the human mindset. Therefore, the difficulties resulting from information disruption might have a negative effect on supply chain operations, which is why many weaknesses may exist in supply chains and why chain members may suffer from information deficiency.

Some companies have noticed those problems and are working to resolve those types of issues. Efforts using various agreements or contracts have been adopted to successfully prevent chain members from keeping information only for their benefit. Many big manufacturers negotiate contracts, which include sharing information provisions about customer demand and product data at the retail and manufacturing levels. Meaningful interactions imply that the manufacturer will benefit from firsthand customer information such as product quality, performance, and postsale services. Similarly, the retailer will also benefit from the original suppliers' information such as product innovation, an update function, and packing design. This result is a typical example of a win–win situation. Those approaches avoid possible outcomes of distorted information integration.

Benefits from appropriate information integration affect SCMs positively. One of the most significant benefits is an engagement of information flow. It allows members in the supply chain to share valuable information and use it for their advantages at no expenses to others. Price setting, for example, is a complex activity, which involves the collection of all the associated supply chain cost information. When the information is used independently somewhere in the supply chain, every chain member tends to keep its information private to maximize its profit rather than share it with its chain partners. Therefore, to better integrate information, one business tendency is to establish a just and objective mechanism. The Arbitration Association of the Republic of China, (a neutral third-party arbitrator organization in Taiwan), which clarifies issues of information integration and verifies that the information is truthfully exchanged and shared for the mutual benefits of the supply chain members is an example of such a mechanism.[8] Everyday low price (EDLP)[‡] has been pioneered and fine-tuned by Wal-Mart across most of its stores is one of the most commonly used practices in business information-sharing settings. The success of Wal-Mart in the retail industry is no doubt the best example to show how critical the information exchange and sharing applies equally and successfully across the supply chain.[9]

Notes

1. Ayers (1999).
2. Morrison and Assendelft (2006).
3. Dell and Magretta (1998, pp. 74–83).
4. Chopra and Merindl (2001, p. 368).

[‡] Everyday low price (also abbreviated as **EDLP**) is a pricing strategy promising consumers a low price. without the need to wait for sale price events or comparison shopping.

5. Hong Kong Trade Development Council, Shippers Today: UPS' Enabling Technologies for the Supply Chain, http://tdctrade.com/shippers/vol28_5/vol28_5_ecom_02.htm
6. Mentzer, Min, and Zacharia (2000, pp. 549–68).
7. Mishra, Raghunathan, and Yue (September 2007, p. 863).
8. Introduction, Arbitration Association of the Republic of China (2007).
9. Lee, So, and Tang (2000, pp. 626–43).

References

Ayers, J. 1999. "Information System Management, Supply Chain Strategies." http://ayers-consulting.com/dload/02-sc-strategies.pdf

Chopra, S., and P. Merindl. 2001. *SCM: Strategy, Planning, and Operation, Part 5, Chapter 13: Coordination in a Supply Chain, 13.4: Managerial Levers to Achieve Coordination*, 368.

Dell, M., and J. Magretta. 1998. "The Power of Virtual Integration: An Interview with Dell Computers' Michael Dell." *Harvard Business Review*, March and April, 74–83.

Hong Kong Trade Development Council, Shippers today: UPS' Enabling Technologies for the Supply Chain, http://tdctrade.com/shippers/vol28_5/vol28_5_ecom_02.htm

Introduction, Arbitration Association of the Republic of China. 2007. Retrieved on September 8, 2007 from http://arbitration.org.tw/english/index-1.html

Lee, H.L., K.C. So, and C.S. Tang. 2000. "The Value of Information Sharing in a Two-level Supply Chain." *Management Science* 46, no. 5, pp. 626–43.

Mentzer, J.T., S. Min, and Z.G. Zacharia. 2000. "The Nature of Interfirm Partnering in the SCM." *Journal of Retailing* 76, no. 4, pp. 549–68.

Mishra, B.K., S. Raghunathan, and X. Yue. September 2007. "Information Sharing in the Supply Chains: Incentives for Information Distortion." *Institute of Industrial Engineers, IIE Transactions* 39, no. 9, p. 863.

Morrison, G.P., and A.V. Assendelft. 2006. "Charting a New Course: The Retail Merchandising-Supply Network." IBM Global Business Services, IBM Institute for *business value*, http://www-935.ibm.com/services/us/index.wss/ibvstudy/gbs/a1024459?cntxt=a1005268

CHAPTER 15

The Future of Supply Chains

In this section we explore some innovative technological advances in the SCM realm. As one can expect, new ideas and innovation continuously emerge in business with SCM being no exception. Some are already exploited, disrupting the supply chain, whereas others are still in a development stage. We examine in more detail hereafter the potential effect of Artificial Intelligence, Robotics, RFID, and Cloud Computing* on SCMs.

Artificial Intelligence-Based SCM

Warehousing management is facing traditional planning and optimization challenges, usually addressed by software and operational solutions. Recently, warehousing material handling side benefited from machine learning capabilities of software engines that could be applied to conveyors.

Bastian Solutions,[†] for example, offers 3D modeling tools allowing the visualization and simulation of how a final conveyor system will operate. Their automated conveyor systems include inline automatic scales and scanners. Other conveyor ancillary equipment comprise various intelligent labelers and strappers, stretch wrappers, and cubiscans automatically obtaining carton dimensions for more efficient shipping options.

---

* In its most simple description, cloud computing is taking services ("cloud services") and moving them outside an organization's firewall on shared systems. Applications and services are accessed via the Web, instead of your hard drive. The services are delivered and used over the Internet and are paid for by cloud customer (your business), typically on an as-needed or pay-per-use business model.
† https://bastiansolutions.com/solutions/technology/conveyor-systems

In Finland, the Zen Robotics team went further by developing an autonomously learning conveyor robot picking prototype whose goals was to be as autonomous as possible by both calibrating itself and improving its picking efficiency with minimal human intervention.[1]

Pega[‡] on the other hand, offers Robotic Automation and Intelligence to assist in optimizing CRM data for better identifying customer needs, wants, risks, concerns, and goals. Pega claims that its Pega Customer Decision Hub allows unlocking customer data and analytics, and using that information to power their AI engine—across any touch point or system—at the precise moment it's needed.

Robotics-Based SCM

Robots are also revolutionizing warehousing operations by supporting warehousing distribution. New warehouse execution systems are creating a broader solution that reduces human intervention, improves flow and process, achieving faster order fulfillment.

For example, robots can use a paper planogram,[§] or an augmented reality tool,[¶] which can direct it to optimal warehouse stock localization. AGVs (Automated Guided Vehicles) have been around in the supply chain and in manufacturing for quite some time. AGVs can be tied to telemetry data, vastly expanding their operational reach. Vision guidance for automated vehicles in industrial automation is a way of achieving independent navigation. A vehicle can adapt to the environment and drive to anywhere it needs to be. Traditional automated vehicles have tape guidance, paint, wires or reflectors that are built into the warehouse infrastructure.

[‡] https://pega.com/products/pega-7-platform/robotic-automation

[§] A **planogram** is a diagram that shows how and where specific retail products should be placed on retail shelves or displays in order to increase customer purchases. Planogramming is a skill used in merchandising and retail space planning. **Planograms** are also referred to as POGs.

[¶] These are the sort of possibilities afforded by the new technology of **augmented reality**. In fundamental terms, the expression **augmented reality**, often abbreviated as AR, refers to a **simple** combination of real and virtual (computer-generated) worlds.

A small robot that can drag products around the warehouse costs $30,000 to $40,000, and can replace five or six people on a rotating shift.[2] The Return on Investment (ROI) is very appealing promising an attractive payback from a piece of equipment that never calls in sick, doesn't have family problems, doesn't quit, and you don't have to replace. It starts to become a pretty attractive proposition.

Augmented Reality (**AR**)** is also happening in the warehouse. The merger of Google Glass and Voice Recognition allows its wearers to communicate with the Internet using natural language voice commands, offering a hands-free and eyes-free operation.[3]

The Internet of Things (**IoT**)†† is another type of emerging technology also affecting warehouses. Today's warehouse is far more than just a facility in which to store inventory. Leveraging the latest supply chain technology and the Internet of Things (IoT), a "smart warehouse" can now serve as a hub to boost efficiency and speed throughout the entire supply chain. From wearables on workers to sensors and smart equipment, Internet-enabled devices and technology can profoundly change logistics management.[4]

Zebra Technologies Warehouse Vision Study finds that 7 in 10 decision makers plan to accelerate their use of technology to create a smart warehouse system by 2020. According to the report, "consumer expectations will drive increased investment in IT and operational functions in warehouses over the next four years as manufacturing and logistics continue to adjust to delivering directly to consumers."[5] Juniper Research states that retailers alone are forecasted to spend more than $2.5 billion in hardware and installation for IoT by the year 2020.[6]

** Augmented reality (AR) is a live direct or indirect view of a physical, real-world environment whose elements are "augmented" by computer-generated or extracted real-world sensory input such as sound, video, graphics, or GPS data.

†† The Internet of things (IoT) is the network of physical devices, vehicles, home appliances, and other items embedded with electronics, software, sensors, actuators, and network connectivity, which enable these objects to connect and exchange data.

RFID-Based SCM

The resurgence in RFID technology has raised it to become a revolutionary element in SCM. RFID ensures that the right goods are available in the right place with no discrepancies and zero errors. It makes the supply chain considerably more precise and improves the efficiency and reliability of the entire chain. As real-time information is made available, administration and planning processes can be also improved. As an example, we choose to describe the processes of the Fast Moving Consumer Goods industry (**FMCG**).‡‡ However, the benefits of RFID in SCM can be reaped also in other industries.[7]

RFID Benefits in Manufacturing

FMCG's market of fast-moving consumer goods is one of the fastest growing world markets. Typically, in a SCM environment, products are counted several times for example, during the manufacturing process' stages of production, washing, and packing. Traditionally, these operations are performed manually. But by using RFID tags and readers, products can be counted automatically much faster because RFID tags can be automatically scanned without having to be in the line-of-sight of an RFID scanner. Furthermore, multiple tags can be scanned simultaneously, which results in cost reductions as labor-intensive tasks can be carried out quicker and more accurately.

RFID tags can store far more information than conventional barcode labels. This information can be used to optimize production processes. Accurate knowledge of the real-time movements of raw materials and the time needed for specific production steps can be integrated into efficient production planning. With the help of RFID, manufacturers can also benefit from increased repair and maintenance information of their machines and equipment. This allows manufacturers to have access to

---

‡‡ Fast-moving consumer goods (FMCG) or consumer packaged goods (CPG) are products that are sold quickly and at relatively low cost. Examples include nondurable goods such as packaged foods, beverages, toiletries, over-the-counter drugs, and many other consumables.

valuable maintenance data. This information helps to plan maintenance schedules more efficiently. Hence, maintenance can become part of production planning and help to prevent costly production breaks.

RFID in manufacturing processes results in less manual work, less production costs, improved visibility, and improved production planning.

RFID Benefits in Warehouse Management

Once production has been completed, FMCG producers pack the products into cartons, and deliver the cartons to the warehouse of the freight forwarder or the buying company. After the cargo reaches its destination, it is not uncommon that it ends up in a warehouse first. Keeping track of a large number of cartons is a very complex as well as time- and labor-consuming process. However, RFID system can be implemented to ease the situation by improving the management of the cargo flow information. In cases where read-write equipment is placed within the warehouse, all in-house movements are additionally registered in the system. This allows for better strategic planning of product locations within the warehouse.

The information that is gathered within the RFID system can lead to significant improvements as the tracking and handling of the products can be done in real time and with great accuracy. In the warehouse, products are easily located as all product movements are tracked and this information is automatically registered in the system. Therefore, a warehouse RFID system offers better visibility of accurate real-time information, faster product locating, and improved loss recording.

RFID Benefits in Tracking and Managing Ship Containers

The most popular way of transporting transport large cargos is by shipping containers. Container transports are often chosen because they ensure safer and more secured transportation, lower costs, standard packaging, and high transport density. Companies that use RFID in tracking and managing shipping containers can track containers within each link of the supply chain. Active RFID tags can be used to track containers in real time in yards and docks. Ultrahigh frequency RFID technology (**UHF-RFID**)[§§] has long identification distance and speeds up identification.

In essence, RFID in container management and tracking offers visibility of real-time cargo movement, improves tracking efficiency, and increase data accuracy.

RFID Benefits in Distribution Processes

Implementation of RFID technology can also add advantages to distribution processes. Usage of RFID will accelerate delivery management, improve efficiency, and increase accuracy during the selection and distribution processes. It will also reduce distribution costs. When products embedded with RFID tags enter a distribution center, the RFID read-write equipment at the entry gate can register the RFID tags, and send the information to the distribution centers' backend system. This information can be used to put the cartons in proper places, sort them quickly and efficiently, and dispatch the cartons to the retailing centers in less time with improved accuracy. Usage of RFID also ensures accurate inventory control.

As the products reach their final destination, they are scanned and registered automatically at the entry point. Therefore, applying RFID in distribution processes speeds up delivery, improves efficiency, increases accuracy, and reduces distribution costs

In summary, supply chain, manufacturing, and the growth of mass customization, with the increasing complexity of everything that is built and delivered in the present marketplace, are going to require automation. One needs to plan with this in mind.

[§§] The read range of passive UHF systems can be as long as 12 m, and UHF RFID has a faster data transfer rate than low- or high-frequency RFID. UHF is the most sensitive to interference, but many UHF product manufacturers have found ways of designing tags, antennas, and readers to keep performance high even in difficult environments. Passive UHF tags are easier and cheaper to manufacture than LF and HF tags.

Cloud-Based SCM

With the explosive growth in supply chain complexity and data volumes, a growing number of companies are trying to find more agile, easily implemented solutions to improve supply chain performance. They have chosen to deploy supply chain planning solutions in the Cloud. Some of the Cloud-Computing models available include Software as a Service (**SaaS**),⁵⁵ Platform as a Service (**PaaS**),⁵⁵⁵ Infrastructure as a Service (**IaaS**),†††️ and Managed Service Providers (**MSP**).‡‡‡️

Cloud-based deployment alternatives remove IT obstacles and accelerate the launching of supply chain initiatives, offering a range of benefits to their users, such as ease of implementation, affordability, reliability, and security through:

Lowering Upfront Costs

Initial capital equipment expenses are reduced and total cost of ownership shifts to a more predictable level.

Optimal Licensing, Hosting, and Servicing Options

The wide variety solutions delivery may be adapted to a wide range of software procurement models or budget levels.

---

⁵⁵ Software as a service (**SaaS**) is a software distribution model in which a third-party provider hosts applications and makes them available to customers over the Internet. SaaS is one of three main categories of cloud computing, alongside infrastructure as a service (IaaS) and platform as a service (PaaS).

⁵⁵⁵ Platform as a Service (**PaaS**) or application platform as a Service (**aPaaS**) is a category of cloud-computing services that provides a platform allowing customers to develop, run, and manage applications without the complexity of building and maintaining the infrastructure typically associated with developing and launching an app.

†††️ Infrastructure as a service (**IaaS**) is a form of cloud computing that provides virtualized computing resources over the Internet.

‡‡‡️ A managed services provider (**MSP**) is most often an information technology (**IT**) services provider that manages and assumes responsibility for providing a defined set of services to its clients either proactively or as the MSP (not the client) determines that services are needed.

Freeing Valuable IT Resource

Cloud-based deployments free up enterprise IT resources to focus on strategic initiatives and meet mission-critical demands rather than installing software updates and performing system administration.

Promoting Business Growth

Freeing resources to support business growth can represent an important competitive advantage.

Accelerating ROI

Cloud deployments often deliver better cash flow and create a positive bottom-line faster than traditional models.

Facilitating Change

Since "the infrastructure is on the Internet," there is no hardware to implement and no software to install, resulting in a flexible upward mobility.

Reducing Downtime Risk

Resiliency and high availability are characteristics of a well-designed cloud-based deployment.

Increasing Security

The fear that storing business data on a cloud server could make it vulnerable to unauthorized access has been lessened by the security track record of hosting providers in securing and ensuring data privacy.

Providing Expert Technology Support Services

The provider's technical personnel are an essential resource for installing software updates, hot fixes, service packs, and version updates in an optimum computer environment.

According to Gartner, cloud computing has reached a sufficient level of maturity to be in its "productive phase."[8]

Notes

1. Kujala, Lukka, and Holopainen (2015).
2. http://jbtc.com/automated-systems/
3. Vlad (2017).
4. Guill (2016).
5. Zebra Technologies Study Finds 7 in 10 Decision-makers to Accelerate Warehouse Technology Investment by 2020, Lincolnshire, Ill. April 26, 2016. https://zebra.com/us/en/about-zebra/newsroom/press-releases/2016/study-finds-increased-warehouse-tech-investment-by-2020.html
6. Retail spend on 'Internet of Things' to Reach $2.5bn by 2020, Hampshire. September 1st, https://juniperresearch.com/press/press-releases/retail-spend-on-iot-to-reach-2-5bn-by-2020
7. RFID Arena (November 2013).
8. Drobik and Michael (2016).

References

Drobik, A., and M. Michael. August24, 2016. "Adapting Your IT Strategy for a Cloud-Dominated Business Application Environment Gartner." ID: G00311186. https://gartner.com/doc/3422117?ref=SiteSearch&sthkw=scm%20in%20the%20cloud&fnl=search&srcId=1-3478922254

Guill, C. June 24, 2016. "Creating a Smart Warehouse with the Internet of Things." https://insights.samsung.com/2016/06/24/creating-a-smart-warehouse-with-the-internet-of-things/

http://jbtc.com/automated-systems/

Kujala1, J.V., T.J. Lukka, and H. Holopainen. 2015. "Picking a Conveyor Clean by an Autonomously Learning Robot." https://arxiv.org/pdf/1511.07608.pdf

Retail spend on 'Internet of Things' to Reach $2.5bn by 2020, Hampshire. September 1st, https://juniperresearch.com/press/press-releases/retail-spend-on-iot-to-reach-2-5bn-by-2020

RFID Arena. November 2013. "Guest Blog, Benefits of implementing RFID in Supply Chain Management."

Vlad, S. July 18, 2017."Google Glass is back from the dead." *The Verge,* http://rfidarena.com/2013/11/14/benefits-of-implementing-rfid-in-supply-chain-management.aspx

Zebra Technologies Study Finds 7 in 10 Decision-makers to Accelerate Warehouse Technology Investment by 2020, Lincolnshire, Ill. April 26, 2016. https://zebra.com/us/en/about-zebra/newsroom/press-releases/2016/study-finds-increased-warehouse-tech-investment-by-2020.html

CHAPTER 16

Conclusions and Recommendations

Business practices have been expanding considerably toward globalization, and business networks have been more complicated than ever. To meet customer satisfaction and strengthen business competitiveness under a fast-changing business environment, a better understanding of how to correctly implement SCM is paramount for business success. As often mentioned previously, SCM deals with various activities involving the flow of material, information, technology, and money from supplier-to-customer and from customer-to-supplier. SCM has become a very powerful business process method proven to make an important contribution to many industry sectors by facilitating business development and growth.

To achieve benefits resulting from proper SCM application, companies have to cooperate with their supply chain partners and end-users effectively. They also need to use their sourcing, manufacturing, marketing, distribution, operation, and purchasing capabilities efficiently by using SCM to ensure that they can increase their profits by delivering their goods and services at the right time, right place, with the highest quality level, and at the lowest cost.

Companies in a successful SCM will eventually increase their market share and enhance their brand reputation. Moreover, because of SCM-related advantages, companies can also attract and maintain their customer loyalty and can count on future business sustainability. As a result, they will increase their return on investment and their profits in the long term.

SCM also carries a crucial and complex integration problem. As competition has forced business models to move from companies to supply chains, more companies are increasingly adopting SCM practices to achieve a competitive advantage and maintain business sustainability. As the needs and expectations of customers are increasing, the importance of finding the right practices for effective business operations is becoming essential. No company can resist this trend without risking its survival.

Although traditional marketing channels may have been regarded as efficient ways to move goods from one place to another, a supply chain can create more business opportunities and effectively reduce operating costs. A repeated highly integrated supply chain execution can drive chain members to overcome long-term complicated problems and secure more compelling core advantages. Consequently, a solid SCM also helps companies to meet target profits and generate greater customer satisfaction. Satisfied and confident customers will come back more frequently and be more loyal.

When advanced systems successfully integrate business processes, sophisticated jobs can be done more efficiently. When information can be exchanged and shared extensively, chain activities and goals can be identified and reached. Once all these objectives are achieved in a supply chain, stakeholders such as investors, employees, and customers will be willing to reward and support those companies. As a result, a good business cycle model will be shaped and its operation will function well repeatedly on the right track of the SCM.

Pressures from globalization and technology advances continue to push companies ahead to survive and thrive. Fierce competition resulting from trade and technological progress is compelling companies worldwide to work closely. Because of marketplace pressures and competition, companies must learn to enhance their capabilities and improve their collaboration in the supply chain to retain customers and maintain profitability. A sound SCM can help reach those goals.

Because of a lack of understanding and expertise, many companies have realized the importance of implementing SCM but often do not know what and how a comprehensive set of supply chain operations operates completely. From a technical point of view, management solutions by I2 Technologies, Manugistics,* Oracle, and SAP, for example, have been developed and applied to provide best support and performances for supply chain activities. Through planning, collaboration, integration, and validation of multilayer operations with these advanced technologies, high-performance teamwork and excellent competitive advantages become available and workable to mitigate competition effects.

From an industrial point of view, one notices that a supply chain is easily affected by business factors, such as market structure, industry type, legal systems, company size, government policy, economies scale, and demand and supply balance. For example, larger companies may require higher levels of supply chain operations because they usually have more complex chain activities associated with bigger scopes of business involvement. Highly contentious industries such as chemical manufacturers and nuclear power plants will require more extensive supply chain collaboration because of their concerns regarding related environmental issues such as pollution, security, health, and regulation. Because the concept of SCM is complicated and involves cooperation between companies, the entire supply chain domain needs to be explored and researched from both the technical and industrial points of view. According to academic research and empirical evidence, proper SCM practice is a preferred road for profitability in business.

SCM strengths of companies can be summarized as:

1. Companies with high SCM integration will achieve a higher level of competitive advantage;

---

* **Manugistics Group Inc.,** founded as STC in 1969, was a company that developed and marketed software applications, principally for resource planning and supply chain management, with offices in over 30 countries. The company was a provider of demand, supply, and transportation planning software, with several very large-scale customers, particularly in the food production industry. JDA Software acquired the firm in July 2006. Source: https://en.wikipedia.org/wiki/Manugistics

2. Activities with higher levels of SCM integration will realize a higher level of operational performance;

3. Processes with higher levels of SCM integration will generate higher levels of organizational efficiency; and

4. Resources with higher levels of SCM integration will yield a higher level of business profitability.

Lastly, the challenges and difficulties of today's business are everywhere. SCM may bring either opportunities or threats. Whether to better manage opportunities and reduce threats, good SCM business practices can be accomplished by applying the following:

1. **Balance both sides of the upstream and downstream supply chain information flow.**
   - *This is an important consideration for achieving mutual gains, which is predominantly relevant at the customers' end; they are often playing a key role in determining the outcome.*

2. **Simplify and integrate operational processes in the supply chain.**
   - *This can help improve performance and increase efficiency against competitors. Companies are encouraged to expand their business and to move more the flow of information throughout the supply chain to achieve success.*

3. **Respond quickly to market changes by adopting flexible supply chain strategies.**
   - *This will strengthen companies and enhance their adaptability and durability. Companies need to develop an elastic SCM system that can also help formulate a set of standards and criteria at an affordable price in dealing with the issues of fast-changing markets.*

4. **Minimize risk and uncertainty by using tools of demand planning and sale forecast.**
   - *This can prevent supply chain members from improper investments or even face bankruptcy. Unpredictable events often show up beyond expectation. Companies, which are involved in a good SCM, will regularly be alert and sensitive to unfortunate*

incidents. Because of well-developed techniques and systems, companies in a well-operating supply chain can lower their potential risks appreciably while taking preventive actions in many business activities and investment projects.

5. **Coordinate and collaborate with supply chain members.**

   • *Supply chain members' coordination and collaboration are becoming the most dominant assets as companies decide to work together as a group. Globalization has been a trend that may influence industries anywhere. Organizations under fierce global competition must focus their efforts on product quality and customer service. Cheaper pricing as a traditional marketing tool is no longer enough to meet market requirements. A comprehensive integration by tighter coordination and collaboration of chain members is important in a global competition context.*

6. **Control variables on costs issues and align them to meet business profitability.**

   • *Companies may consider losing their cost advantage in the short term when expecting to secure best market share or to provide comprehensive customer service. However, establishing a well-designed supply chain will improve operational efficiency and increase productivity. As a result, even though costs may escalate in particular areas, the shift to better supply chain networks can control many intangible variables such as time-consuming events or tedious processes that will eventually reduce costs indirectly in other areas, resulting in higher profits.*

7. **Update systems by starting with smaller initiatives.**

   • *SCM is an important tool comprising many systems, software, equipment, and procedures. Companies in the supply chain need to adopt long-term technological solutions deployed in their modules rather than implementing a general system redesign. If, for any reason, the supply chain programs must be upgraded or re-engineered, a better way is to take actions systematically as separate projects. The results will not merely save operational costs and time, but also increase systemic flexibility and stability.*

8. **Focus strategies on resources integration in the supply chain activities.**
   - *This is critical to ensure high-quality cost-reduction and time-saving implementation. Resources are always limited and need more care in waste management. Effective integration of external and internal resources can help facilitate organizational functions and enhance business values.*

9. **Emphasize greening issues on supply chain execution.**
   - *The supply chain must turn the business direction from market-oriented focus to environment-friendly issues. Companies are starting to perceive increasing concerns in environment protection from communities, society, and government. Energy efficiency improvements, procedure simplification, and greenhouse gas emitting reduction will gradually contribute to superior environmental protection.*

10. **Offer comprehensive service and technical support.**
    - *This is more important than the product itself. Creating business value is a likely by-product of effective supply chain performance. In current business settings, companies working as separate entities cannot provide high-quality individual practices to meet increasing market demand and customer requirements. Apart from products, they must also provide sufficient service and support.*

Companies applying SCM need to pay careful attention and deliberate thinking more than on just technical issues. Companies in any industry must step out of their practices and operations.

The trend toward SCM started decades ago, and is increasingly moving to almost every industry and spreading out virtually in every corner worldwide. To catch up this business trend and to sustain market competitiveness, companies must understand the benefits SCM can deliver.

SCM has a decisive positive influence on business development and prosperity.

About the Author

Dr Milan Frankl held technical, marketing, and management positions with IBM Canada. He later joined the Desjardins Cooperative Movement as Director of Clearing Systems. While with Desjardins and through the Canadian International Development Agency (CIDA), he spent some time in Latin America, implementing a generalized financial infrastructure project for the Latino-American Cooperative Movement (COLAC) out of Panama City. Next, he joined CGI as a Director of Consulting services and partner where he participated in a large number of strategic projects in the private and public sectors. After moving to Victoria in the early 90s, he became, respectively, CFO, President, and CEO of several hi-tech Canadian businesses. He is presently a Professor of Business with University Canada West (UCW), a member of Global University Systems (UK).

Index

OTHER TITLES IN OUR SUPPLY AND OPERATIONS MANAGEMENT COLLECTION

Joy M. Field, Boston College, Editor

- *Contemporary Issues in Supply Chain Management and Logistics* by Anthony M.Pagano and Mellissa Gyimah
- *Understanding the Complexity of Emergency Supply Chains* by Matt Shatzkin
- *Mastering Leadership Alignment: Linking Value Creation to Cash Flow* by Jahn Ballard and Andrew Bargerstock
- *Statistical Process Control for Managers, Second Edition* by Victor Sower
- *Sustainable Operations and Closed Loop Supply Chains, Second Edition* by Gilvan Souza
- *The High Cost of Low Prices: A Roadmap to Sustainable Prosperity* by David S. Jacoby

Announcing the Business Expert Press Digital Library

Concise e-books business students need for classroom and research

This book can also be purchased in an e-book collection by your library as

- a one-time purchase,
- that is owned forever,
- allows for simultaneous readers,
- has no restrictions on printing, and
- can be downloaded as PDFs from within the library community.

Our digital library collections are a great solution to beat the rising cost of textbooks. E-books can be loaded into their course management systems or onto students' e-book readers.

The **Business Expert Press** digital libraries are very affordable, with no obligation to buy in future years. For more information, please visit **www.businessexpertpress.com/librarians**. To set up a trial in the United States, please email **sales@businessexpertpress.com**.

www.ingramcontent.com/pod-product-compliance
Lightning Source LLC
Chambersburg PA
CBHW062024200326
41519CB00017B/4919